Values in social policy

Radical Social Policy

GENERAL EDITOR

Vic George

*Professor of Social Policy and
Administration and Social Work
University of Kent*

Values in social policy
Nine contradictions

Jean Hardy

Routledge & Kegan Paul
London, Boston and Henley

First published in 1981
by Routledge & Kegan Paul Ltd
39 Store Street, London WC1E 7DD,
9 Park Street, Boston, Mass. 02108, USA and
Broadway House, Newtown Road,
Henley-on-Thames, Oxon RG9 1EN
Printed in Great Britain by
Redwood Burn Ltd, Trowbridge and Esher.

British Library Cataloguing in Publication Data

Hardy, Jean

Values in social policy. – (Radical social policy).
1. Social policy
2. Values
I. Title   II. Series
361.6'12   HN29   80–41949

ISBN 0 7100 0782 5

CONTENTS

Contents

Preface

The true problems of living ... are always problems of overcoming or reconciling opposites – E.F. Schumacher, 'Small is Beautiful', 1973, p. 89

This book is based on the lectures I have developed over four years' teaching on two master's degrees, of Applied Social Studies, and of Public and Social Administration. My intention is to analyse the conflicts in which people working in the welfare state are enmeshed, to trace some of the roots of the arguments, and so on to help people fear conflict and uncertainty less. The basic assumption is that there is no value-free way of working in the welfare state, or indeed of living one's life, and that a person entrusted to some extent with other people's lives has obligations both to know his or her own values and their significance in action, and to be able to understand some of the forces in society that deeply and dramatically affect values in general. Working in the welfare state is not only a matter of technique, even in jobs that have a technical content; there are moral, philosophical, political and social questions underlying every decision and every personal encounter.

Most legislation, and most administrative practice springing from legislation, is a compromise between conflicting values and forces within society. These essays offer an examination of political, philosophical and sociological contradictions which underpin the services that we have: the welfare services, particularly the social services, are constantly referred to in the book to substantiate the general argument – working in a situation of conflict is inevitable for those in these services. The more any individual understands this, the more realistically can that person operate

within the system towards the values which seem to him or
her of fundamental importance.

The nine contradictions examined in this book are, in
order of presentation:

1 Authority versus liberation
2 Representative versus participatory theories of
   democracy
3 Needs versus resources
4 The family: the basis of society or the root of all its
   problems?
5 Bureaucracy versus professionalism
6 Theories of decision-making: rationality versus
   negotiation
7 The individual versus the community
8 Equality versus freedom
9 The personal versus the political

The analysis of needs and resources occurred first to me,
and the original version of this essay was published in 1970
as an article in the 'British Hospital Journal and Social
Services Review'. (1) The work on the nature of authority,
particularly in relation to bureaucracy and professionalism,
was part of my original doctorate, the main body of which I
abandoned because I became more interested in the limits of
authority than in its actual nature. The decision-making
study was part of some research I undertook with others on
work in children's departments in 1968-71. The family is
a necessary interest for any sociologist who is also a social
worker, and teaching social workers, as I am. The relationship between freedom and equality is an inescapable
question for all who consider themselves socialist, as I do.
The issues concerning community, the idea of fraternity,
participation and the nature of democracy have sprung from
involvement in community work over the last few years. The
list of contradictions is endless, and personal.

The final chapter, on the personal and political, is different from the others because it is an attempt to penetrate
nearer to the heart of the contradictions we see all around
us. Like all the other chapters, it uses material from
sociology, political philosophy, social policy and social
work. The question haunting this chapter is more obvious
than those in the other eight; it is at the heart of my
impulse to give the lectures and write this book: are the
structures and attitudes engendered by Western society too
deeply corrupting for us all, or, faced with our society's
many deep faults and virtues, is it worth while fighting

within the system for alternative vision of what life could be for people?

I am, in this book, as I was in the lectures, attempting to work out a viable freelance critic's stance to take as a person and a worker in this society. It is important for people working in our society to know where they stand and to be able to explain their position to others. I am not attracted to being a 'card-carrying' member of any group, even those critical of the many alienating features of our present society; this book is an attempt to face the many contradictions that we live with and to make some sense of them for myself.

Acknowledgments

With thanks to the students at Brunel University and London
University who attended the lectures on which this book is
based, particularly for all their forthright comments of
every description; my colleagues in the congenial Department of Government at Brunel; my friend, Jo Klein, for her
frank and careful editing at the penultimate version and for
her encouragement to write the book in the first place; Vic
George, for his sympathetic guidance; my niece, Elizabeth
Rimmer, who compiled the bibliography; and Christine
Lorenz, Ruth Cook and Marie Heard, for their typing of the
various editions of the lectures and the chapters.

1

Authority versus liberation

This intellectual liberation from the inevitable may be one
of the most important next steps we have to take –
Barrington Moore, 'Injustice: the Social Bases of
Obedience and Revolt' (1)

Authority is related to the idea of legitimation: what is it
proper to do. Both the person in the subordinate position
and in the superior recognise that the transaction between
the two is rightful, and rests in a larger social system of
order. Authority is essentially about order and about the
way that value systems work; they work because we believe
in them, because there is an internal consistency between
the institution which promotes the authority relationship and
the beliefs of the people involved. A system of authority
therefore is where socialisation, beliefs, values, superior-
subordinate relationships or structural systems come
together and need to be understood in relation to each other.
For any social system to work harmoniously there needs to
be a consistency between institutions and personal beliefs;
where that consistency does not exist – which is usual in our
society – there is scope for rebellion, disorder, an underlife, change.
  Authority is essentially about how values are sustained
with a considerable degree of consent: it is the way any
ordered society works. Durkheim's work is particularly
preoccupied by the relationship of social forces to morality,
and to the nature of the individual. The concept of authority
analyses that relationship : (2)
    the ideas and sentiments that are elaborated by a collec-
    tivity, whatever it may be, are invested by reason of their
    origin with an ascendency and an authority which cause the

1

particular individuals who think them and believe in them to represent them in the form of moral forces that dominate and sustain them.

Authority is tied up with the idea of 'the right', of values which ought to be followed and which individuals accept and believe in.

Clearly authority can be accepted at different levels. Probably many people living in Britain at the present time would accept the general and pervasive values of 'liberal democracy' and hold these very dearly, maybe even in Durkheim's sense of 'ascendent', but even given this, there would be other levels where a person would dispute the values of a particular institution and the authority of the people running that particular system. A person rejecting the basic values of the entire system, and therefore rejecting its authority, its legitimacy, would be likely to opt for complete withdrawal or for revolution; someone accepting the basis but refusing to accede to the legitimacy of particular institutions, values or people would be more inclined to a reformist frame of mind.

Those accepting the social system as given, or not thinking about such questions, or those who feel or are powerless to change anything, are those who make it work as it is. Probably there is a part in all of us, however questioning, which accepts large areas of 'the given', at least in practice. People in any society grow up with some acceptance of authority; we all have been small children and subject to both authority and power in our formative years.

Barnard (3) explains this acceptance of a wide range of authority by the idea of a 'zone of indifference', 'a margin of trust' which is necessary just for ease of living.

'Ease of living' is not, however, the major moral issue in the unthinking acceptance of authority. Social thinkers in the last decade or so have been motivated to investigate the human capacity to go along with barbaric regimes without protest. Adorno, (4) Fromm (5) and Bettelheim (6) studied the reaction to the Nazi government, Fromm in the nation at large and Bettelheim in a concentration camp. Milgram (7) carried out a series of well-known experiments in the early 1960s on peoples' readiness to obey the authority of an expert and found this to be remarkably and frighteningly high. The question of obedience to authority and the conditions for revolt has been the subject of Barrington Moore's latest writing. (8) It is strange that we usually accuse a person who reacts against a particular system as having 'problems with authority'; probably a far more devastating propensity of the human being in general is the real problem with authority: the likelihood that most people will accept almost any situation or system as given, and find a way to live with it. Adorno's work is interesting because it so clearly ties in the 'authoritarian personality' with the social institution, showing how through the family, the education system and the overt power structure of society the person is formed to fit in. Bettelheim demonstrated how many of these authoritarian traits were present in the victims of the Nazi concentration camps and helped to keep these structures going – in fact, prisoners were often harder on each other than were their guards. Fromm comments on the 'fear of freedom' in individuals, a fear of taking lonely personal responsibility and a wish to escape into the crowd, however oppressive. The subordinate's position in any authority – not power – situation is one we are just beginning to understand and see the significance of.

Authority must be distinguished both from power and from influence. Power exists where there is threat of sanction, of force or of the control of resources; here a belief in the legitimacy of the superior is not necessary – a person can be forced to do what another person requires by strength or by the threat or actuality of sanction. This distinction between authority and power is a most significant one, even though many situations contain elements of both authority and power – one has only to think of the relationship of a teacher to a pupil in a school, or the status of a country 'bobby' to realise the intricacies of the personal and role position. Again, influence is very different from authority, for there is no superior–subordinate relationship implied in influence. Hannah Arendt sums up these distinctions very clearly: 'if authority is to be defined at all ... it must be in contradiction to both coercion by force and persuasion through arguments': what a person has in common with the one obeying 'is the hierarchy itself, whose rightness and legitimacy both recognise'. (9)

We can therefore pinpoint several characteristics of the authority situation which must be present:

(a) a superior–subordinate relationship recognised by both

(b) within a value system that both accept, and

(c) which is therefore regarded by all parties as rightful and legitimate.

It is, in fact, difficult to imagine a society holding together without some pattern of authority, as human beings tend to create institutions which are nearly always hierarchical, and also tend to regard some individuals with more respect than others, either inside institutions or regardless of institutions. However, to see that authority relationships are universal in human societies does not mean that one has to accept the particular system pervasive in one's own society, especially as the authority system is intimately linked with, and represents, the values underlying it.

At this point it is useful to say that the authority of one person in relation to another can exist in general, or can vary between two individuals in different areas of life - say expertise in a particular subject, or the authority a particular job or relationship gives. You may be a professor but I may be a better sportsman. This would be the case in the most equal society.

It is helpful to consider the different kinds of authority, particularly as they exist in the welfare state, in more detail. Weber's analysis, (10) made at the beginning of this century when the strength and characteristics of capitalism were already clear, is still the classic taxonomy. He distinguishes between traditional, rational-legal and charismatic authority. Traditional authority exists where practice and belief are hallowed by time; the class system draws largely on this kind of authority, especially where middle-class doctors, teachers or social workers administer to working-class patients, pupils or clients; the technical role is then reinforced by tradition, in so far as the patient, pupil or client accepts the superiority of the middle-class 'normal' culture.

Traditional authority in this society, is, however, residual when examined against the pervasiveness of rational-legal authority. This concept recognises that both in private firms and public bodies people work together, usually in large bureaucratic systems, on the basis of contract. This contract is either implicit or explicit in the actual employment of a worker, and the vast majority of us are employed. Public bodies are generally devised to administer some aspect of the law - a particularly obvious fact in the welfare state. A person working in the welfare state therefore derives his authority through his contract with his employing body - ultimately the state - and is contracted to carry out the administrative processes of the law. His authority is both justified and limited through that employed position. The legal system carries authority in itself because it is, at least in theory, a system set up and sustained by the decisions of the elected representatives of the people.

The authority of the state is, however, very close to power, as Joel Handler points out in one of the few analytic works on the social services. (11) State provision is backed by the police and ultimately the army, and has control of many resources, so that power is fundamentally mixed with authority in virtually every service. A probation officer has the direct authority of the court system and the police behind him; on the other hand a social worker in, say, a child guidance clinic typically has to rely on the authority he carries with the parents and children, as he has very little power over resources and very few sanctions. A physiotherapist is in a similar position to the child guidance social worker, but a consultant physician or surgeon has considerable power over resources and great potential sanctions over patients.

Charismatic authority, Weber's third kind, rests in the 'leader', or in the attractive draw of a framework of values. The charismatic leadership of an Ivan Illich, an Enoch Powell or a Herbert Marcuse can carry authority for the adherents of the message, but this force carries only potential authority against the strength of the rational-legal structures in which our lives are lived and which the capitalist economic system underpins.

There is one further type of authority not included in Weber's original analysis, but which is very important in the welfare state, among other places – that of expertise. As Rhodes writes – 'many people look to the sciences rather than to religion as the source of truth. They accept the authority the more gladly because it passes the most convincing of tests: "it works".' (12) The scientific theory of knowledge is dominant in this society. Expertise is particularly important in the authority of the professional and the semi-professional in the welfare state, again in so far as people accept the skill of the professional and are prepared to believe and see that what he does really does work.

Friedrich (13) defines the authority that professionals carry as 'superior knowledge or insight' depending on 'the potentiality of reasoned elaboration'. Both the authority and the power of knowledge are important here – control of resources need not only be in terms of money or goods, it can also be about knowledge and expertise.

We can see then that, in the welfare state, different institutions and the different individuals within them possess different kinds of authority, power and influence. A doctor
who is also a consultant could have the authority of his
expert knowledge, combined with a significant position in a
hospital hierarchy within the health service, together with
the traditional authority of his status and class for some of
his patients, with even some charismatic authority thrown
in: with that accumulation of authority, he will hardly have
to depend on his power. A police chief will be in a very
different structural position, with a very strong degree of
rational-legal authority, considerable expertise but with a
most explicit power base. It would in fact be possible to
analyse the structural position of all officers of the welfare
state in this way, and more attention will be given to this
conceptual framework in the chapter on bureaucracy and
professionalism. All the people working within the welfare
state, or subject to its workings as a consumer, are involved with both general and specific systems of authority, and
need to develop a critical understanding of their own position and of the position of others with whom they work: this
understanding would be of the basis and <u>also the limitation</u>
of their own and others' authority.

CRITICISM OF THE PRESENT SYSTEM OF AUTHORITY
WHICH IS BASICALLY A CRITICISM OF THE PRESENT
VALUE SYSTEM AND THE WAY THAT IT WORKS

We can take two fundamentally different attitudes to our
present society – either of basic acceptance or of deep
criticism. The society is a capitalist liberal democracy
modified by a large welfare element; it is a society in which
for most people it is more materially comfortable to live than
in most societies people have known before; in Britain it is
also relatively free of governmental force, and there is an
atmosphere of considerable if limited toleration of difference.
On the other hand, the society is grounded in values that
lead to and depend upon inequality of goods and of power, to
competition as a considerable force in human relationships,
to consumerism, to the failures as well as the strengths of
the nuclear family, with an endemic alienation, isolation and
powerlessness for many, and to the relative destruction of
the environment. It is a consideration of our values and
the authority and power systems that enable these values to

work that lies behind all the contradictions discussed in
these chapters.

It is interesting that in some research by Stephen
Cotgrove expectations of catastrophe or cornucopia were
bound up with structural position in society. Cotgrove re-
ports that most people are both accepting of the society and
optimistic about it: (14)

they appear to be cornucopians and not catastrophists.
The central values of industrial society are endorsed by
most of us through upbringing. The business community
overwhelmingly adopts a cornucopian view.... Cornucopians are genuinely puzzled over how anyone could pos-
sibly see things the way the catastrophists do. Catastrophists, in turn, are exasperated at the apparent
stubborn blindness of the optimists. Opposing doctrines
about society and the environment confront each other
incomprehensibly. There is increasing frustration at
the possibility of working through the political institutions,
which are seen as dominated by a coalition of unions,
industry and government in pursuit of growth.

Contradictions exist on many levels, but the issue of basic
acceptance (cornucopians in Cotgrove's study) or basic dis-
truct and fear (catastrophists) of our present way of living is
deeply felt and pervasive.

It is against these two opposing points of view, which
represent opposing pictures of reality in society, that I put
forward some of the trenchant criticisms of what we have
that have been offered in the last decade or so.

Marcuse, a voice from the Frankfurt school, and a man
most influential in the protests of the 1960s, sums up some
of the implicit values of our society: (15)

a comfortable, smooth, reasonable, democratic unfreedom
prevails in advanced industrial civilisation, a token of
technical progress. Indeed what could be more rational
than the suppression of individuality in the mechanisation
of socially necessary but painful performance; the concentration of individual enterprises in more effective,
more productive corporations; the regulation of free competition among unequally equipped economic subjects; the
curtailment of prerogatives and national sovereignties
which impede the international organisation of resources.
That this technological order also involves a political and
intellectual coordination may be a regrettable and yet
promising development.... Independence of thought,
autonomy, and the right to political opposition are being

deprived of their basic critical function in a society that seems increasingly capable of satisfying the needs of individuals through the way in which it is organised.... All liberation depends on the consciousness of servitude, and the emergence of this consciousness is always hampered by the predominance of needs and satisfactions which to a great extent have become the individual's own. Consumerism which dictates needs for individuals is a political quite as much as an economic phenomenon.

The authority of the official bureaucracy has been equally attacked. Ralph Miliband begins his influential book: 'more than ever before men now live in the shadow of the state. What they want to achieve individually or in groups, now mainly depends on state sanction and support.' (16) His analysis is in a direct line from Marx, writing in the mid-nineteenth century. Charles Reich extends the criticism of the authority of a bureaucracy which is in some significant way, irresponsible: (17)

The first crucial fact is the existence of a universal sense of powerlessness. We seem to be living in a society that no one created and no one wants.... The structure of the administrative state is that of a hierarchy in which every person has a place in a table of organisation, a vertical position in which he is subordinate to someone and superior to someone else ... when an entire society is subjected to this principle, it creates a small ruling elite and a large group of workers who play no significant part in the making of decisions.

All these writers are arguing that liberty is suppressed by the particular use of rational–legal and expert authority in a technological society. The decision–making system we have generated treats resources, including knowledge, as secret, and the vast majority of the population is employed by or implicated in the enormous decision–making machine, either in the market or in the state system. What is more, most people, as they must, believe in this system – which is the reason that it more or less works. Our minds and personalities as well as our earning capacities are implicated: (18)

Elites, ruling classes, bosses, adults, men, caucasians – superordinate groups generally – maintain their power as much by controlling how people define the world, its components and possibilities, as by the use of more primitive forms of control.

The strength of authority is needed to convince people that

they are living in a good society: that they are free as
individual freedom is one of liberal democracy's overt
values. In the libertarian view, however, all of us working in the welfare state are fooling others as well as ourselves by colluding in Marcuse's 'repressive tolerance', by
accepting a particular society which places systems above
people, and where material comfort is paramount.

LIBERATION

Liberation, unlike freedom, is reactive: it is reactive
against a particular authority. It depends, as Marcuse
writes, 'on the consciousness of servitude': consciousness
and awareness have always been qualities linked with
liberation from oppression. And in the case of the liberation movements in the sixties and seventies of the twentieth
century the forces of liberation are directed against the
'reductive humanism' (19) of the technological materialist
society, 'the absurd affluence of middle-class America ...
where the evils spring simply from the unrestricted pursuit
of profit.' (20)   The thrust of liberation movements began
in America in the mid-1960s but were equally significant in
Europe, where the characteristics of 'normal' society are
similar.
The movement was not only about structures of society but
more particularly about what happens to individual people –
the disappearance of souls into the machine. The most
helpful analysis of the movement is contained in Charles
Reich's 'The Greening of America', first published in 1970.
He describes the three kinds of 'consciousness' contained in
the three historically distinct world-views existing currently in contemporary America. He is implicitly using
Kuhn's (21) notion of the paradigm, the basic assumptions
involved in any 'normal' culture which distinguishes that
culture from the one before and which is based on criticism
of the anomalies of the previous framework. We have in
our society radically different views of what we see before
us, though of course the consciousness of this is greater
among those rejecting the normal culture than among those
'cornucopians' who accept it.
These three kinds of consciousness determine the personal characteristics of individuals under three systems of
authority. Reich's Consciousness I predates much of our
present society, and to my mind is similar to the world-view

held by the English Conservative Party which is currently
being put into practice. The authority contained in this
mode is traditional, in Weber's terms. The fundamental
tenets are a belief in the Puritan ethic in the way you live
your life and the way you think other people should live
theirs; hard work, achievement, technical freedom to do
what you want within a clear code of personal morals, the
importance of the 'small man', the acceptance, indeed the
approval, of inequality, the resistance to state interference.
It is the consciousness appropriate to the early nineteenth
century, to the beginning of the industrial revolution and is
basically liberal, placing great importance on the individual
in the liberal sense of possessive individualism. There are
forces of course within Consciousness I that react against
the present power of the state, but other values such as the
importance of the market system, the machinery of profit
are fully acceptable to this view.

Consciousness II is the reality of the role-player, the
person who fully accepts and believes in the values of the
technological society, and accepts without demur its great
material advantages. It is the rational-legal caste of
mind: (22)

> An established hierarchy and settled procedures are seen
> as necessary and valuable. Achievement by character
> and hard work is translated into achievement in terms of
> meritocracy of education, technical knowledge and posi-
> tion.... Consciousness II people are tremendously
> concerned with one another's comparative status....
> Consciousness II man adopts, as his personal values, the
> structure of standards and rewards set by his occupation
> or organisation.

A further frightening characteristic is that such men or
women refuse to accept personal responsibility for the
things their organisation does, so that they are able to
work without problems in, say, the arms trade or advertis-
ing. Such people are all the time trying to dominate experience, not live with it, so nothing really has that much
effect on them. They have no other standard of reality or
authority except the given, for that is how they have been
brought up in their families, in the schools, in their employment. Reich ends by writing: (23)

> Consciousness II is the victim of a cruel deception. It
> has been persuaded that the richness, the satisfactions,
> the joy of life are to be found in power, success, status,
> acceptance, popularity, achievements, rewards, excel-

lence and the rational, competent mind. It wants nothing to do with dread, cause, wonder, mystery, accidents, failure, helplessness, magic. It has been deprived of the search for self that only these experiences make possible. And it has produced a society that is the image of its own alienation and impoverishment.

Writing now at the time of the General Election in April 1979, it seems to me that both the Labour and the Conservative Parties hold this world-view strongly and the Liberals weakly. The trade unions are as much dependent on the technological system as are the straight capitalists, and use the same weapons, are as interested in power, status and differential.

Liberation from these forces is really difficult for the individual person and for structures. A brilliant asset of the capitalist system is its ability to incorporate everything, and at the point of writing it seems that much of the vivid hopeful protest of ten years ago has already been incorporated, so that the only difference now resulting from that movement is a modification of the style of institutions and people.

But what is Consciousness III, which is at this time the force of liberation from the present authority? It is first of all an effort to develop a good relationship with yourself, and a preparedness to accept yourself, not to be afraid of the 'dark side' as a basis for accepting others in all their differences. Taking oneself seriously carries with it the necessity for taking others as seriously, always putting the human interest before the efficient working of systems. Politically this had led to an emphasis on human rights, attempting to define the limitations of our present system of authority. With this is an acceptance of full personal responsibility for what you do, and an obligation to consider and sometimes reject the values that are required and encouraged in society.

This is close to a reflexive approach and style of living. Alvin Gouldner described reflexive sociology in his influential book, 'The Coming Crisis of Western Sociology', recognising that 'knowledge of the world cannot be advanced apart from the sociologist's knowledge of himself and his position in the social world, or apart from his efforts to change these.' (24) A reflexive view of living relates the inner world of the person to the structures outside, and takes neither for granted. The personal problem of this definition of liberation is that you become an outsider in 'normal' society. This not only rejects the fraternal values of the movements of the sixties, but it makes it impossible to work as a fully committed member of the institutionalised welfare system unless you honestly find it easy to work within its framework without much question. And this makes it difficult to work with integrity with consumers of these services whether they be 'clients', students or patients. It is far easier to work within a system if you fully accept it. Bill Jordan compares the situation of present-day social workers with those a hundred years ago: (25)

> the notion that the authentic expression of the true self is that of the outsider, who resists society's demands on him, is more difficult to reconcile with ideas of constructive intervention in the lives of others than the Victorian notion of personal integrity and social cohesiveness.

The patronising and narrowing influence of our present system of welfare, which involves those who have offering services to those who have not, means that the services may be wanted but they carry with them conditions that are questioned by some consumers and some workers: 'personal freedom and liberation must resist the encroachments of helpful people, especially those who represent the official ethos of participation in the formal world.' (26)

The basic idea of the liberation movement is that, in the matter of personal freedom, you can find only your own: it cannot be given to you. This puts all workers in the welfare state in a really difficult position, as Jordan points out. Given the nature of bureaucratic and professional roles, and the hierarchical organisations in which most of us work, all you can do is alter your style if necessary, and regard authority as springing not only or not predominantly from the organisation which employs you but also from the person you are there to serve. In some jobs this is easier than others. It is easier in this sense to be a university teacher than to be a local authority social worker, a worker in an open participating agency than in one that guards its status and its secrets. It is easier in the former circumstances of each pair to keep a critical edge to one's mind and feelings, to keep that personal consciousness that Dostoevsky is writing about: 'though I stated ... that consciousness, in my opinion, is the greatest misfortune for man, yet I know man loves it and would not give it up for any other satisfaction'. (27) The cost of completely believing in the authority of any social system as given, is to lose or never to achieve that personal consciousness which is at the heart of being a free person.

Other values follow that of taking human beings, including
yourself, seriously. It becomes necessary for institutions
to serve people, and not the other way round. Individual
rights are spelled out. The satisfaction of people at work
and at leisure becomes predominant: profit is merely a means
to this end and must be put in its place. Competition
becomes unimportant if it leads only to stress rather than to
fulfilment. Formal status is seen as a negative value.
Goods are valued only to some extent; but as soon as it is
clear that for one group to have goods means that others are
poor, goods become a burden. The need for certainty
becomes irrelevant. There is a remarkable similarity to
early Christianity, or indeed to any similar movement critical of an established order.

In addition, poetry, feeling, physical pleasure, love are
recognised as powerful needs. The spiritual and the mysti-
cal have more meaning than the material. The personal
becomes political, the political personal.

All these values contradict those existing in 'normal'
society. They are not supported by the normal structures,
and do not fit into the existing patterns of authority. There
is a strong feeling that life can be, and ought to be, better.
People convinced by these values have formed radical
groups in professions and organisations, and have tried to
live their lives working one system while believing in
another, or have tried and perhaps succeeded in modifying
their working environment, or have sought to work and live
with like-minded people, or have left the normal work system
or just used it: they have done all the things in short that
any minority group does in a hostile or indifferent environment.

When Reich and Roszak wrote their books at the beginning
of the decade, it looked as though the whole world could be
changed by a change of consciousness. Since then there has
been a world economic recession, heavy inflation and a
closing of ranks. Community work used to look radical and
in fact produced some of the most telling critical literature
in the Community Development papers, (28) but now many
community workers are quietly pursuing their own individual
and often isolated work, often working contentedly for the
state. There is a strong conservative movement among
students. Many doctors, teachers and social workers are
unhappy about the implications of the job they are doing and
the society they are living in, but can see no alternative.
There is still a strong Marxist tradition in England, but that

often seems as rigid as the normal system: it does however
provide a consistent critical thrust.

On the other hand, one of the most interesting developments has been the continuation of the liberation idea among
women's groups, gay groups and black people. It is now
possible for children in care to form their own group to look
after their own really neglected interests. It has now
become feasible for many hitherto submissive groups to
become vocal and alert. And this must have some impact on
the majority.

A rather hopeful book has recently been published – in
1977 – on changing values over the last decade, carefully
supported by surveys. The book is 'The Silent Revolution'
by R. Inglehart. Two quotations will give the main
message: (29)

One aspect of the change in values, we believe, is a
decline in the legitimacy of hierarchical authority,
patriotism, religion, and so on, which leads to declining
confidence in institutions. At the same time, the political expression of new values is facilitated by a shift in
the balance of political skills between elites and masses.

The final chapter begins: (30)

beneath the frenzied activity of the 1960s and the seeming
quiescence of the 1970s, a Silent Revolution has been
occurring that is gradually but fundamentally changing
political life throughout the Western World. This book
has described two major aspects of this revolution: a
shift from overwhelming emphasis on material consumption
and security towards greater concern with quality of life;
and an increase in the political skills of Western publics
that enables them to play a more active role in making
important political decisions.

In the later chapters of this book it is possible to see,
for instance, how participatory methods of democracy
struggle to exist in a representative system, or how the
family is variously considered as an institution. Most of
the roots of the contradictions I am describing lie in the
ideas of liberation and criticism of our present society that
do not seem to have died in the last fifteen years but are
slowly working through the system. The potential is enormous still because the ideas would require us all to live
quite differently from the way we do now and define our
reality in a quite other way. Many of the protests and the
movements have been incorporated. Whether the changes
will be merely of style (and that in only some areas of life)

or whether the ideas will be more potent than that, we can only see. There is certainly no way for Western societies to stay still. The economic system continues to be the dynamic that drives us most fundamentally. The question remains, though, whether the shifts in consciousness springing from the last fifteen years will lead to a revolution in consciousness and economies that will fall into Kuhn's definition of a change of paradigm, of a new perception of the world, of a different definition of 'normal', of a 'shift of vision'. (31)

2

Representative versus participatory theories of government

In the last ten years or so, participatory decision-making has become very popular, but those advocating participation have often been disappointed when attempts have been experienced as less than successful. People tend not to turn up to meetings; vociferous members often monopolise the floor; cliques form and the majority of people fall again into apathy.

These tendencies are more understandable when we realise that participatory and representative theories of democracy are significantly different from each other; they rest on different models and distinct histories, and lead to quite contrasted structural and decision-making patterns. They also require dissimilar attitudes of mind. We try to practise participation, with attitudes developed through many years of using the representative style of decision-making, only to realise that structure and attitudes must have an internal consistency for any human institution to work effectively.

Part of the confusion arises because both modes are consistent with the idea of democracy; they are in fact different methods of practising democracy. Democracy is defined plainly by Holden as 'a political system of which it can be said that the whole people, positively or negatively, make, and are entitled to make, the basic determining decisions on important matters of public policy'. (1) The basic authority lies with the people, and the key to the definition is the actual decision-making power.

Participatory decision-making was the original, direct style, being appropriate for the relatively small city state of ancient Greece. A huge population and the forces of industrialisation have produced the more indirect version – representative democracy. I would like to describe and distinguish between these two models in theory and in practice, and consider some of the implications of the differences between them in the welfare state today.

We are all used to the representative mode. Its features are well analysed by Pateman: (2)

The characteristically democratic element ... is the competition of leaders /elites/ for the votes of the people at periodic, free elections. Elections are crucial to the democratic method for it is primarily through elections that the majority can exercise control over their leaders through loss of office ...

the decisions of leaders can also be influenced by active groups bringing pressure to bear during inter-election periods. 'Political equality' in the theory refers to universal suffrage and to the existence of equality of opportunity of access to channels of influence over leaders....

The level of participation by the majority should not rise much above the minimum level necessary to keep the democratic method (electoral machinery) working; that is, it should remain at about the level that exists in the Anglo-American democracies.

This system is relatively efficient in terms of time; Pateman quotes from Bachrach that 'such a model of democracy can be seen as one where the majority (non-elites) gain maximum output (policy decisions) from leaders with the minimum input (participation) on their part'. (3)

Such a system relies on a considerable degree of passivity, then, in the majority of people: a relatively silent majority (that familiar phrase) is actually desirable and necessary. In the words of J.S. Mill, 'the people ought to be masters, but they are masters who much employ servants more skilful than themselves'. (4) In this theory the authority of the amateur 'masters' on the one hand and the skilful 'servants' on the other (if this is indeed a true description of either), rests on very different bases: the citizens face the 'skill' of the elected representatives on the one hand and the bureaucracy on the other.

The term representative has several meanings, sometimes understood as being related to characteristics (the standard 'housewife', for instance, as a criterion used in commercial decision-making) and sometimes related to views (where the person elected is given a mandate). In both local and central governments, a person is elected according to views held and policies advocated - often according to political manifestos - but once in power the elected repre-

sentative is part of the machinery for governing the whole
country or local authority.

As A.H. Birch points out, 'members of parliament ... are
elected representatives whose first duty should not be to
promote the interests of their electors but to promote the
interests of the nation as a whole, according to their judgment of what is best.' (5) The opposition, too, is mobilised
in a similar bloc, ready always to defeat the government
party in power.

The problem of the relative degree of conflict or consensus
is differently handled in the two methods of democracy.   In
the representative system, 'the role of the people is to produce a government', (6) whose job is to rule: leadership 'in
this competitive struggle for political power' (7) is the
accepted dynamic force.   Consensus is not therefore needed
because the most popular party wins and, from then on,
holds political power.   It is only when the opposition forces
become in time stronger than the majority party that the
power swings to an alternative political group.   Conflict is
therefore expected in the system, and controlled within it.

The characteristics of the representative mode, therefore,
are as follows:
- (a) elected representatives, jointly governing the
    electorate;
- (b) universal suffrage, elections being held at regular
    intervals: people elected therefore accountable to
    the rest;
- (c) pressure groups, with access to the representatives,
    pressing for particular claims between elections;
- (d) in the short term, the majority of the population rela-
    tively silent indicating a considerable degree of con-
    sensus, real or apathetic;
- (e) large 'skilful' administrative groups responsible to
    the elected representatives for carrying out pro-
    grammes, ensuring some of the skill necessary for the
    elected 'servants', and ensuring continuity during
    change of government (the civil service, local govern-
    ment bureaucracy, boards of nationalised industries);
- (f) alternative government waiting in the wings, always
    ready and motivated to mobilise oppositions: an ex-
    pectation of overt conflict in the long term;
- (g) minority interests (theoretically) secured through
    opposition party and pressure groups;
- (h) explicit structure appropriate for governing method of
    decision-making; e.g. a constitution: decision-making

tends to be in representative committees with a constitution: importance of due process: confidentiality of
much decision-making.

Representative government is linked particularly to large
nations and to large local units. We elect representatives
when there are too many people to gather in one place to
make decisions. The fewer the people actually taking part
in the decision-making process, the more likely it is that
quick decisions will emerge. And the larger the organisation, the more necessary it is for an explicit structure to be
agreed on.

In this nation of fifty million people, we are used to the
structure of representation at many levels of the society.
It is not only used nationally, but in work-places, in trade
unions, in local government and in most interest and pressure groups.

By way of contrast, a participatory democracy would produce a very different world, and indeed, in general, we
would have to have very different attitudes of mind to make it
work. It is a direct system of decision-making, 'one characterised by a high proportion of decisions being made by
the people actually assembled together', (8) where the populace not only votes on issues but also initiates policy.

Participation derives from ancient Greece - it is the
'classic' theory of democracy. Ray Lees states the characteristics of the method quite briefly: (9)

in democratic Athens all the important decisions were made
directly by the face-to-face assembly of all citizens.
Leading offices, like magistrates, were filled not by election but by lot, so that any citizen had as good a chance as
any other to be selected; most public officials held their
offices for one-year terms and were not eligible for re-
selection. Even the Athenian equivalents of modern court
trials were conducted either directly by the general
assembly or by large groups of citizens chosen by lot.
The two prime qualities of Athenian democracy, then,
were popular control of public decisions and maximum
public participation in making decisions and in holding
public office.

It should be noted, of course, that Athens had only a few
thousand free citizens: women and slaves were not included
in the above arrangements. It was actually possible for
all free men on occasion to gather in one place.

In Athens, the Assembly (of all) met monthly; there was a
right and a duty to attend. A Council of 500 was chosen by

lot - 50 men from ten tribes. The Council prepared business and dealt with emergencies. An Inner Council of 50
was in session for one-tenth of the year; the Chairman was
chosen daily by lot. (10)
    Such a system is quite unlike our present efforts at par-
ticipation which are essentially, as yet, partial. R.G.
Brown (11) makes a useful distinction between the three
kinds found in our present welfare system. There is syn-
dicalism, rooted in Cole's guild socialism, which relates to
worker control in industry and work organisations: the
doctors have always had political power, both in forming the
National Health Service in 1946 and then in running it, (12)
and an attempt, full of difficulties, has been made in the
1974 reorganisation to include nurses, administrators and
other relevant groups in the decision-making process. In
the health service, the education system and the social services, the general ruling is that the more prestigious and
powerful the profession or trade group the more weapons it
has, of course, to gain power within the organisation,
towards syndicalist participatory decision-making.
    Pressure for more client involvement is the second from
participation has taken: in social work, for instance, foster
parents have formed their own groups, children in care have
formed Who Cares? groups, (13) and old age pensioners, the
disabled and neighbourhoods have developed as pressure
groups in relation to the services provided for them, but,
more importantly, have attempted to influence both policy-
making and decisions within the organisations. This participatory tendency Brown describes as a 'popularist movement having its roots partly in legalistic concepts of individual rights, partly in the social work ethic about the need to
help clients become independent, and partly in the middle-
class consumer association movement.' (14)
    The final arm of the movement is the general push towards
general community development, linked with community
action, to boost the power of people in local areas vis-a-vis
central and local government.
    Thus, within our welfare services, which are governed
basically through representative democracy with a very
heavy component of bureaucracy, we have a considerable
push towards participation: while it is a long way from the
classic model, it is operating on several different levels
within the welfare state. Participation is essentially about
power in making decisions rather than about style, and it is
a movement that calls for definite inroads into the major

system of decision-making and will not be satisfied with only therapeutic measures. Consultation is not true participation.

The participatory system either assumes the idea of a common good 'the obvious beaconlight of policy, which is always simple to define and which every normal person can be made to see by means of rational argument' (15) - an assumption that Schumpeter criticised and, in criticising, questioned the whole basis of the direct system; or, in the modern attempt, it assumes conflict of views and interests being fought out at every level of the process. Clearly, however, participation would be far more viable in a more homogeneous social system. There would have been a considerable communality of interest between the free (not slaves) men (not women) in ancient Greece that could not be found in a modern Western democracy. There would seem to be a direct correlation between the homogeneity of society and the viability of participatory systems - unless the skills and awareness and implications of the system were very greatly developed in the participants. Representation, relying as it does on the assumption of conflict and the passivity of the majority of the population, can cope with real clashes of interest in a way that is impossible in a truly participatory system.

To my mind, there are four main questions raised about the feasibility of the participatory system in today's society - a society that, unlike that of ancient Greece, is large, industrial, capitalist, hierarchically organised, with a strong class system and differential economic power, and with all the people - rich and poor, men and women - potentially involved in the decision-making process.

The first question is about the nature of men and women - is the human being a political animal? Do people in this society want to be concerned in the decisions most affecting them and are they competent to do so in this highly complex society? The second question, the reverse side of the first, is whether (or maybe how far) the decision-making process can be made public and participatory in a society where confidentiality is regarded as a virtue, and where powerful bureaucratic positions and expertise are jealously guarded.

The third issue is the one about size. Is participation in the true sense of the word - where decision-making power is concerned - really feasible in a nation of fifty million people, or indeed in the very large formal organisations

that employ most of the populace?   And finally there is a
great problem in a participatory system about the protection
of minorities, and, indeed, the whole construction of an
appropriate framework to allow for and to accommodate conflict comparable with the one developed in the representative
mode.

IS MAN A POLITICAL ANIMAL?

In this society, we tend to make a firm distinction between
public and private life.   There is a tendency to regard
private life, based in personal relationships and family, as
being more 'real', or at least as the situation in which
people prefer to spend their time.   It is the relatively unusual person who spends much 'private' time in 'public'
affairs.

Rousseau, in his development of the Athenian theories of
participation, supposed that citizens would regard participation in public affairs as being part of a full life rather
than an optional extra. (16)

Rousseau's entire political theory hinges on the individual
participation of each citizen in political decision-making
and in his theory participation is very much more than a
protective adjunct to a set of institutional arrangements;
it also has a psychological effect on the participants, en-
suring that there is a continuing interrelation between the
working of institutions and the psychological qualities and
attitudes of the individuals interacting within them.

It is the relative absence of the participatory cast of mind
that has been responsible for much of the disappointment
mentioned at the beginning of the chapter.   G.D.H. Cole
argued fifty years ago that the majority of people had been
'trained to subservience' in families, schools and employment.   This is, after all, what the representative system
requires.   Participation grows by being practised, in all
these institutions.   Participation has within it the model of
a 'participatory person' - independent, feeling equal in a
basic sense with others, wanting to exercise rational judgment about issues outside himself and his immediate concerns, practised at joining with others in common tasks,
geared to thinking he or she has a right to join in public
decision-making and reasonably confident that his or her
decisions will be effective.   Participation is a learned
activity.   It is a learned activity that gives equal weight to

man as a political and public animal and as a private individual; in fact, the political element is probably the more
weighty, and this for the modern English person - unlike the
ancient Greek - would be a considerable shift in self-image.

This learning to participate has been a constant theme in
community work, and is one of its basic values. As S.M.
Miller and Martin Rein comment, using one example as sum-
marising this fundamental belief: 'People change as they
try to change their world. While the Harlem experiment
with community-based schools created deep conflict between
professionals and consumers, it also changed the aspirations
of adults and increased the educational achievements of
children who participated in it'. (17)

To live in a participatory rather than a representative
democracy would mean that most of us would have to become
rather different people.

We would need to value fraternity, responsibility for all
others in society, rather than individualism and family
loyalty; we would believe we had more power - and we would
actually have to possess it; we would wish to take part
seriously in many general issues; and we would spend a
greater proportion of our lives in doing all these things.

CAN DECISION-MAKING BE MADE PUBLIC AND
PARTICIPATORY?

Some of our more recent attempts at institutionalised participation have been greeted with less than enthusiasm. Community Health Councils are not participatory in the full
sense of the word, as they have no decision-making power
about the use of resources - a point graphically commented
upon by Shirley Williams when she described them as 'the
strangest bunch of administrative eunuchs any department
has yet foisted on the House, a seraglio of useless and
emasculated bodies'. (18)

Bureaucracies and experts are reluctant to yield their
power. In the health service, groups from t he community
have been offered monitoring and consultative functions
rather than actual clout in making decisions. Within the
health service, the somewhat pseudo-participatory principles that have been used in the 1974 reorganisation have
been put into operation most clumsily. (19) Our institutions
are based on principles of bureaucracy and expertise, and
of course are structured with vested interests. We would

not only have to have a significant shift in personal attitudes
to accommodate the participatory mode fully, we would need
institutions with a radically different format.   What we have
now is a range of somewhat vulnerable participatory groups
existing within bureaucratic or representative organisations,
at odds with the parent structure, either actually or potentially.   There are attempts to incorporate some of the spirit
of participation into existing institutions, enabling people to
take part in decisions most affecting themselves and encour-
aging a greater openness in decision-making, with less
emphasis on expertise, especially when the decision to be
made is one about values rather than techniques.

Adah Kay, in her study of the attempt to incorporate participatory principles in local authority planning, points out
in another area of the welfare state, how partial is the
attempt.   She writes: (20)

> Although, on the face of it, the public living under an
> assiduous local authority can be involved at fixed states
> in the planning process through various communication
> and public relation exercises, in effect, ultimate control
> lies with the professional and the politician.

She comments further on the class bias of this very class-
ridden society: 'Involvement of the working class in planning
rarely happens'. (21)

PARTICIPATION AND SIZE: IS PARTICIPATION
POSSIBLE IN A NATION OF 50 MILLION, OR IN A
FORMAL ORGANISATION EMPLOYING THOUSANDS OF
PEOPLE?

The argument of this chapter is that the difficulties of
grafting one system – participation – onto another – representation with a heavy component of bureaucracy – have not
been sufficiently realised.   This point is made even more
clear by G.D.H. Cole, when he writes in 'Democracy Face
to Face with Hugeness', (22)

> democracy can work in the great states ... only if each
> state is made up of a host of little democracies and rests
> finally not on isolated individuals, but on groups small
> enough to express the spirit of neighbourhood and perso-
> nal acquaintance.

In other words, participatory (or representative) democracy
starts from the bottom, from the family, the neighbourhood,
the school or college, the organisation of departments in

local government, the work-place, to neighbourhood councils and to the idea of fraternity.

Schumpeter believed that it was only on this level, of their own experience, that people could make decisions, otherwise 'the sense of reality is so completely lost': (23) the average man knows about his immediate surroundings, at home and at work, 'the things that are familiar to him independently of what his newspaper tells him'. (24) Because participation in Schumpeter's view could never be realistic beyond the local level, he believed, the participatory theory is impractical in modern society.

Cole's belief, on the other hand, was that both in workplaces and in the nation as a whole a participatory system could work, but only if it were firmly based throughout society. It is only marginally feasible to try to graft it on, as we do at present – in the welfare state, or in industry as is proposed in the Bullock Report on democracy in industry. (25) But even if a radical and considerable shift in attitudes and institutions occurred, there is still a logical problem about size: fifty million people cannot gather together in one place, and a representative element would have to be brought in – but then it was – in Greece – for short-term decision-making.

THE PROBLEM OF MINORITIES AND OF STRUCTURELESSNESS

Within representative democracy, we try to ensure minority rights and individual autonomy by a complex set of rules; in the court system, through committee procedures, through the formal structure of local and central government. These procedures may seem pedantic, routinised, a bar to creative action at times, but they are a guard against the too great tyranny of the majority, the rich and the powerful. These safeguards are more difficult to envisage in the participatory system. Unless everyone became a 'participatory person', relatively strong, articulate, unafraid, then the lack of structure could easily lead to a crowd situation, the powerful could ignore the powerless, a rule of the majority could ignore minority interests. One certainly cannot be sure that the morally virtuous and the rational would win in any system, particularly as there are no 'objective' means of saying who these are. Most charismatic leaders, including

Hitler and Mussolini, have used participatory crowd support
to gain power. Most political theories rest on a view,
explicit or implicit, of human nature; the participatory view
assumes man to be both ultimately rational and ultimately
good, in groups and crowds as well as individually. We may
be, in the long run, but recent history – probably all history
– casts some doubt on our short-term ability to act well
without many checks, balances and structures.

The weakness of the lack of structure even in little groups
is pointed out well in a recent women's liberation
pamphlet (26) – most women's groups attempt to operate as
participatory organisations. The writer maintains there is
no such thing as an unstructured group and, indeed, any
study of group dynamics leads to that very firm conclusion;
if there is no formal structure, the person who knows the
implicit rules, who knows most people, who most fully shares
other people's values, is the strongest. Power then
becomes capricious, leads to a 'star' system and to charismatic leadership. And without some system of action, a
participatory group remains impotent: 'unstructured groups
may be very effective in getting women to talk about their
lives: they aren't very good for getting things done.' The
problem of participatory decision-making in large structures
and in structures concerned with the decisive action have
certainly not been solved.

The representative system has a similar fundamental dif-
ficulty in terms of democracy: it tends to maintain the status
quo, to maintain the established rich and powerful where
they are. This causes less fuss, especially if the people
in the weaker positions – the poor, the black, the women,
the poorly educated – accept their positions, but the problems to do with the implementation of democracy are no less
great.

CONCLUSION

One of the problems for us at the present time is that we are
between two systems. The representative model is the
dominant one, with participatory styles of decision-making
common particularly at local level.

The participatory model involves more skill, more awareness, more commitment and clarity than the representative
model if it is to work at any level in a large social structure.
The individual would have to be a person <u>wanting</u> to partici-

pate in public affairs, and skilled in it: everyone would
have to know definitely what he stands for. Participatory
decision-making would need to start at the small group or
small social institution and be practised constantly. New
structures would have to be devised, as the same safeguards
in organisation have not yet been developed. The ideal of
participation is more ambitious and more hard work than that
of representation in truly trying to fulfil the aim of 'government by the people'.

If we were able to analyse more clearly the potentiality
of the mix between representative and participatory theories,
with more credence being given to participation than
Schumpeter was able to give, we might be able to make a
more viable system out of the contradictions. If we became
more political as citizens, were able to practise real
decision-making in the family, the school and the local
environment, would we be able to make such inroads into the
representative system that a real change in theory and
practice could be brought about? Can political power really
be brought in by people significantly at the local level? Can
people grasp more clearly the national decisions that have
got to be made so that we can do more than choose our
leaders and then support or oppose them?

The long-standing opposing systems of democracy, and
their relation to freedom, authority and equality, have to be
re-assessed in each period of time. Due to the thrust of
the participatory movements from the 1960s, which seem,
according to R. Inglehart (27) - and indeed according to
common experiences - to have made an inroad into the representative mode, this seems to be the time to work again at
this area, so that the theory can encompass present practice. (28)

3

Needs and resources

Needs are potentially infinite: resources are always
limited and therefore scarce – Roy Parker, Social Administration and scarcity: the Problem of Rationing (1)

The relationship of resources to needs is particularly
striking in our current economic difficulties, but the same
basic dilemma exists in all welfare provision, and affects
the working of all other values. The struggle is ecologi-
cally as well as socially based, and was clearly seen by
Malthus at the beginning of industrialisation. In the last
ten years or so, we have become more morally aware of
this economic relationship. We see only too clearly the
scarcity of natural as well as industrial resources, and of
the tendency of industrialism to rape the earth. We see
also the moral caution we must employ in thinking of human
need as being 'infinite' without qualification: the question of
whether we in the rich nations should limit our desire for
more and more is seriously and urgently discussed.
    Need is often seen as physical: for food, clothing, shel-
ter to support our physical existence. Even in this area of
need, however, relative judgments become quickly necessary. We have been trying to define the basic minimum of a
person's primary physical need throughout this century.
Booth, in his investigations at the turn of the century, found
it necessary to make a distinction between primary and secondary poverty – the requirements necessary to keep a
human being alive, and those which would enable him to live
in his particular culture.
    Even basic physical needs vary from country to country,
according to climate, physique and diet – and, more important, according to the standard people have got used to.

In the March 1979 edition of the periodical 'Action in Distress', four rights (a concept clearly related to need but with very different political connotations) are spelled out for the people of the under-developed countries: the right to enough food to eat, the right to clean water to drink, the right to simple medical care when sick, the right to the opportunity to support themselves and their families. These are needs not met in many countries but are needs which people in Britain, and in most rich nations, would tend to take as self-evident. In industrialised societies, however, the 'unplanned relentless drive of capitalist development continually generates new needs ... numerous "social problems" from the middleaged redundant to the victims of urban development to the thalidomide children, can be associated with rapid economic and technological progress'. (2) Need, as poverty, is always relative, though the wish to implement basic minimum standards for all people is a constant motivation in the writing about the concept.

But beyond these physical needs, as the psychologist A.H. Maslow pointed out through his 'hierarchy of needs', (3) there are other requirements that any person has. People need conditions conducive to mental health, self-respect, dignity, love, a sense of identity, the opportunity to use one's intellect, happiness. These conditions clearly do not exist in many - if any - places in the world today. But these more subtle needs could be as important as the physical ones in the provision of welfare services. In the services offered by education, health, housing, social services, it is impossible to consider physical needs only. Even in housing, where there is the most obvious tendency to consider only physical conditions, there has been a steady and sometimes most vociferous pressure against placing small children in high-rise flats because of the effect this was discovered to have on their social and emotional development.

Policies can, in fact, be based on definitions of emotional need. In 'Child Care and the Growth of Love', John Bowlby wrote, (4)

What is believed to be essential for mental health is that the infant and the young child should experience a warm, intimate and continuous relationship with his mother (or permanent mother-substitute) in which both find satisfaction and enjoyment.

This has been a basis for policy in the social services: fostering has been preferred over residential care for very

young children; a family system of residential care has been
generally set up in the nurseries that do exist; social workers have been trained to support the relationship of the
mother and the very young child. The statement has been
subsequently modified in Rutter's work, (5) and is currently
under some attack because of the imprisoning effect it can
have on the natural mother of a young child, and because of
its cultural bias in what is now a multiracial society, but
its effect, as the statement stands, on policy and practice
is still strong.

Similar statements on the quality of life, on the intellectual and emotional needs of people, can be found in the educational services in particular, and of course in the mental
health services. Need is a most complex concept.

This complexity has been captured and tamed by Jonathan
Bradshaw in a different way in his taxonomy of need, (6)
though the definitions are somewhat static. He distinguishes
between four types of need. First, there is normative
need, which is related to the idea of a desirable standard, a
standard usually defined by an expert (such as Bowlby) in the
area, but generally adhered to by most experts. Work has
been carried out in this country and the USA on social indicators to define need, though this merely puts the problems
we find qualitatively into quantitative form. (7) In the different welfare services, minimum standards of provision
are implemented to conform to normative definitions of need.
In housing, for instance, the Parker-Morris standard of
1961 is adhered to in council houses so as to define not only
the quantity but also the quality of housing required in a welfare state. In health, a basic provision of mother and
baby care before and after birth is routinely considered
necessary. In education, all children should be educated
'according to their age, ability and aptitude', however loose
that recommendation. In the social services, all disabled
people have the right to be at least registered under the
Chronically Sick and Disabled Persons Act, 1970, with
hopefully some other services being a corollary of the regis-
tration. Normative needs leading to normative basic services are recognised in the provisions of the wlefare state.

Bradshaw's second definition is of felt need - in other
words, want. This may or may not manifest itself in some
action by the person with the want. This is therefore very
different from the third kind of need, which is expressed
need: demand. Demand is what most welfare services that
cater for minorities, where no alternative definition of need

is available, respond to. The referral rate or demand is what most social service intake teams regard as need: we would all recoil quickly if we regarded want rather than demand as being the appropriate concept of need. Demand not only requires more effort than want on the part of the person expressing the need, it is also more likely to be influenced by the services known to be available. Known resources are, in fact, likely to some extent to determine demand: there is no point in applying to the social services for a car, or for happiness. Social security and the health services also respond, selectively, to demand. Both individual demand and people grouped together in pressure groups - for example, claimants' unions - may affect the proferring of the services.

The final need in Bradshaw's list is comparative need - need, as Benn and Peters write, for 'things that most other people have got', (8) which is how most of us frame our thinking about need. Runciman's work on reference groups (9) is helpful here, in trying to understand how people build up their picture of what they need, and with whom they compare themselves. This fourth definition, and the second definition, of want emphasises the personal, subjective and yet culture-bound idea of our own need that most of us carry. That this definition can get out of all proportion to resources in a given society is the import of Marcuse's argument in 'One-Dimensional Man'. He writes critically of the affluent society which creates false needs for commercial purposes; in what sense do we 'need' washing machines, large cars or cosmetic surgery?

From the foregoing discussion, we can see that the welfare state is essentially concerned with need. There is usually both a physical and a psychological element in the definition. Social workers are concerned with mental health and happiness as well as with adequate money. Teachers are involved with growth and creativity in their pupils as well as with basic skills. Doctors must pay attention to the psychological as well as the physical state of their patients. Social policy is to do with the quality of life as well as minimum provisions, though there are many moral problems about individual rights centring upon that issue.

Each of the services in the welfare state is concerned with a rather different meaning of need. The health services, for instance, operate largely on demand, but the situation is complicated because health care in Britain is a

right as well as a need. We are all entitled to it. The
issue then becomes the quality of health we come to expect,
and the mediation of that expectation with the discretionary
decision-making of administrators and professionals within
the service. The 1976 DHSS pamphlet, 'Sharing Resources for Health', points out the relativity of expectation, but
also its main trend: 'there is ample evidence to demonstrate
that demand for health care throughout the world is rising
inexorably'. There are, however, some quantifiable data
too on the attempts to examine the need for health care – for
instance, the number and proportion of old people in any
community can be ascertained and, what is more, predicted
with some accuracy. Minimum standards of health care can
to some extent be measured and known. Major difficulties
about need tend to arise above that minimum level when technological advance may meet personal need at a high cost and
then must be rationed – for instance in relation to dialysis
and kidney transplants. There is also the over-riding
question, raised by Illich (10) among others, as to whether
the need is for the treatment of ill-health, or for a service
and a society designed to promote positive health, with pre-
vention of ill-health as a major concern.

In education, too, the quantitative need is known, at least
for children and young people, and again the basic questions
are to do with quality and objectives rather than quantity.

The personal social services are in the interesting
position, in contrast to housing, education and health,
of being a minority service, where it is far from likely that
everyone within a particular category will claim that service. One could certainly argue that health and the education of children falls within Wilensky's and Lebeaux's (11)
definition of an institutional service within the welfare state
which 'sees the welfare services as the normal "first line"
functions of modern industrial society'. The social services, however, are far nearer to the residual idea, where
the 'social welfare institutions should come into play only
where the normal structure of supply, the family and the
market, break down.'

It is assumed in this society that families will support the
children born to them, and will also care for the parents
when they become old. It is the 'odd' situation, on this
assumption, that produces a child who needs to come into
care, or an old person who requires the care of an old
people's home. Most people earn money through the market
system and, once again, it is assumed that many people will

substantially pay for their own times of trouble. The task
of the local authority social services departments is to
administer the legislation on behalf of the minority groups
for whom the market and family systems fail. Demand then
becomes the important criterion of need. The Seebohm
Report (12) somewhat vaguely put forward an alternative
version of this, advocating 'the development of community
identity and mutual aid', the service being available to all.
But until such a model becomes a reality anywhere, the
social services remain residual, meeting demand and very
much dealing with a minority, particularly the poor. The
same is true of supplementary benefit, though in this service
the idea of need is much more intertwined with the notion of
rights; the service is even more stigmatised and thought to
apply to a very small minority in peculiar circumstances.

In fact the needs of individuals are throughout the system
limited by the demands of market forces. Ian Gough, in his
recent book, puts this clearly: (13)

an education policy designed to meet the needs of children,
however they are defined, will sooner or later come face
to face with the unwelcome reality of the labour market and
of the uncreative, degrading nature of much modern work.
A policy to beautify our cities and plan the physical environment will encounter not only a nest of private property
rights, but behind these the blind forces of the urban law
and property market, and behind these the free movement
of capital between regions and even countries.

It is at this point, when considering need and how it can
be met, that it is most easy to perceive the basic contradiction in the very existence of the welfare state. Reformers
of mainly socialist persuasion have struggled for the benefits embodied in the welfare programme. But that same programme is the other side of capitalism, essential to its survival in the twentieth century: 'the welfare state can be
envisaged both as functional to the needs of capitalist development and as the result of the political struggles of the
organised working class'. (14) It is this contradiction
which places critical social administrators in such a difficult position: social workers may be assisting individuals
and at the same time assisting a system they find pernicious:
a social administrator going on strike may be making a decisive political point but at the same time may be harming the
people he or she is there to serve.

A further contradiction is that even thinking about need at
all is a limiting process. 'Meeting minimum needs' does not

seem to be about a good life, but only about survival. It is in a way a conservative concept, static and often patronising. And used as a concept on its own, with no reference to the social setting, the systems of power and distribution of wealth, it gives a false sense of neutrality about the idea. But need is so widely used as a tool and is so undesirably linked to basic notions of an acceptable standard of living that some discussion of the idea itself seems inevitable.

Resources available to meet need also come from the two economic systems of the society – the market system and the welfare system. The two systems work on very different bases, rest on different values and lead to different consequences. As Coates and Silburn reiterate, (15)

the truth is that the welfare and the market principles are irreconcilably in conflict with one another, and at no point in time is there a declared truce; there is no gentleman's agreement as to the proper province of each, no honourable observation of agreed demarcation boundaries. On the contrary, the two methods of distribution remain in a perpetual and dynamic state of opposition.

That the market system is much the stronger and more basic is a view maintained strongly by J.H. Galper in a recent study of the American social services. The market constantly undermines the welfare system: (16)

The positive social concerns and the efforts to meet human needs that are represented by the better impulses of the social services are undermined by the forces which the social services sustain and reinforce in the society at large.... The problems in the welfare state and in the social services can be traced consistently to their embeddedness in and indebtedness to the 'master institutions that caused the problem', as Gouldner has aptly called them.

This also means that many people at the top of hierarchy in the social service must be more attuned to the 'master institutions' than to the people whose need they are ostensibly set up to serve.

This is very obvious too in the housing system, where houses are obtained through the forces in both systems, but where the actual cash comes from the market, in the shape of building societies: local authorities are heavily indebted to these societies.

Resources exist in two main forms, either in visible capital, of goods or money, or in services – the skill and knowledge of staff, time available, and services rendered.

Most resources are tied up well in advance, in buildings
whose use is already designated or in staff who are already
employed. Flexibility is usually extremely limited, both in
terms of these commitments made physically and also in relation to the heavy financial indebtedness of government to the
commercial market world.

Most of the money and assets are tied up already. Residential accommodation for the elderly, for instance,
accounts for almost a third of the total overall social services department spending. (17) Also, flexibility of resources is limited by the attitudes of administrators; people
within local government tend to work from last year's
budgets, making incremental changes rather than working
from first principles. (18) Resources are then much more
likely to be spent in relation to demand as the definition of
need, and spent also in a very circumscribed area in new
ways.

Resources spent on the social services have increased
enormously since the Second World War. Now social services take through their hands nearly 30 per cent of the
national product: (19) 'social service spending has risen
from 4 per cent of GNP in 1910 to 11 per cent in 1938 to 28
per cent in 1976'. (20) Personal social services, though
small proportionately, have shown the greatest proportionate
growth. (21) This increase in resources for social services
is echoed throughout the industrialised world, and is related
to population changes, relative costs, extended services,
different definitions of need, most particularly changes in
political balance and also to the relatively slow growth of
the GNP. (22)

Four methods are used to pay for these resources: taxes,
charges, borrowing and credit creation. These methods of
finding money all have considerable political import: high
taxes are believed to be a disincentive to the competitive
materialist attitude required for the working of the full
market system; charges grate against the concept of univer-
salist services, such as the health service, and sometimes
require means tests for those services regarded as essential; borrowing is a system used most obviously by local
authorities for the building of houses – but 'it gives rise to
continuing annual charges for interest and redemption of
debt, and hence to a need for extra current revenue to meet
them'. (23) It also, as Cockburn points out, makes local
authorities beholden to the workings of the private
market, (24) which, combined with their dependence on cen-

tral government for funds, now makes the local authority
system very much a satellite of market and central political
forces.

One way of highlighting the very piecemeal method of
reconciling need to resources is to take a look at regional
variations, much of which are very difficult to explain on
any rational basis, and demonstrate more clearly than anything else the unknown and probably accidental relationship
of the two. Regional variation is very important in practical terms because of what Bleddyn Davies calls 'territorial
justice'. (25) The fact that it is the variations that are
unintended is demonstrated in the 1976 'Sharing Resources'
document about the health service which declares its
'underlying objective ... as being to secure, through resources allocation, that there would eventually be equal
opportunity of access to health care for people at equal
risk'. That this is not now the case can be demonstrated
in Table 1, which, though it is now ten years old, illus-
trates most graphically that local conditions, local resources, local administrative values, deeply affect the way that
resources and need (usually defined as demand) are related.

Table 1 Payments made under 1963 Act Section 1 in 1967

Payments made overall were £198,000.

Six authorities can be coupled to see variations:

Birmingham	pop.	1,101,990	spent	£2,357 ⎤
Coventry	pop.	333,830	spent	£5,250 ⎦
Oxford	pop.	109,350	spent	£2,302 ⎤
York	pop.	105,550	spent	£35 ⎦
Lewisham	spent most –			£8,000 ⎤
Burton on Trent spent	–			£6 ⎦

Source: Answer given in Parliament, 'New Society',
         8 January 1970.

In summing up this section on resources, therefore, we
can see that resources are limited, unevenly distributed,
often tied up inflexibly in buildings or in methods of thinking,
subject to political pressures and are, of course, grossly
affected by a situation of heavy inflation. The resources so
far discussed are those of the state, and to some extent
those of the market system. Whether resources in society

not measurable in economic terms as demonstrated for
instance by Titmuss in 'The Gift Relationship' can be
brought into play to meet need is another question again –
though it is clear that virtually everything in this society is
greatly influenced by the market system: any process that is
not so influenced is going counter to the major pressures of
society.

Rationing is the technique by which needs and resources
are reconciled. Roy Parker (26) in his seminal article,
describes the major forms of rationing in the welfare state.
It can be seen in the practices of (a) deterrence – where the
service is obtainable but the means of getting it very un-
pleasant – as was seen par excellence in the Poor Law – and
is still seen in some social security offices, for example;
of (b) restricting eligibility – the terms of reference for
help are defined narrowly, and people may be passed from
one service to another. This is arguably the most justifiable form of rationing as it is open and explicit, but it is
difficult to put into operation when the terms of the service
are wide open to different interpretations; of (c) delay – a
common way of rationing, perhaps involving making waiting-
lists and hoping that by the time a person's name comes to
the top the problem will have solved itself; of (d) not giving
information so that people do not know to what rights they
are eligible, or making the service so complicated that
people are bemused; and of (e) dilution of service – little
time being spent on each case or situation, so that any possible effectiveness is at a minimum. As Parker points out,
'the worst kind of rationing is unacknowledged', and he comments that unconscious rationing – which all these methods
may be – is 'often to the detriment of the weakest and most
needy'.

I would add one further method, (f), which is defining
need by the resources available. An education authority,
for example, can acknowledge that it has, say, sixty malad-
justed children because it has a school with that number of
places. In this sense, resources may be synonymous with
'need'. In fact, 'need' is so relative and potentially enormous that it may often be seen entirely in relation to the
resources that any particular agency can provide.

In the different systems of rationing on particular cases,
discretion is very important. Discretion can be seen as an
administrative system of reconciling different and contradictory values and forces, including the economic problem of
needs and resources, at ground level and privately.

Howard Glennerster's study (27) of systems of rationing and discretion in the American and English social services, paying particular attention to the explicitness and centralisation of decisions, is an excellent study of the forces discussed in this chapter.

The basic dynamic of needs and resources looks entirely economic. But, on further examination, the issues raised are as political, as moral, as contradictory, as the other dichotomies considered in this book. The way resources relate to need affects questions of freedom and equality, is fundamentally involved in the style of decision-making prevalent in the system, and highlights the workings of the market and the welfare mechanisms.

4

The family: the basis of society or the root of all its problems?

The sociological imagination enables us to grasp history and biography and the relations between the two in society. That is its task and its promise - C. Wright Mills, 'The Sociological Imagination' (1)

We are a greedy, murderous, cannabalistic and sexually excitable species. This is clear to anyone who has ever taken care of a 2-year-old over an extended period of time - A.R. Roiphe, The Family is Out of Fashion (2)

The family has a very special place among the relationships which through conscious and unconscious mechanism influence the psychic character of the vast majority of men.... The family ... sees to it that the kind of human character emerges which social life requires - M. Horkheimer, 'Authority and the Family' (3)

It sometimes seems that, in the family, all the contradictions of society gather together in one vortex. It is the median between the individual and society, between the inner private world of the self and the demands, attractions and horrors of the society around. It is where the intimate biography of the individual meets the forces and changes of history. The family is the social institution where it is most clear that attitudes and structures must have some consistency with each other for the set-up to work - that the structure of roles must promote appropriate attitudes, particularly in children, and that attitudes will support or undermine the authority of the structure. Feelings are often at their strongest in the family - the institution promotes the most murders and perhaps the most tenderness -

and reason struggles with the force of these feelings. It
is the subject of most of our novels and much of our social
science – art and science focusing with absorption on the
same small significant area. Sociology and psychology,
Marx and Freud, fight over the interpretation of its meaning
in wider terms. The insider who has accepted the prescri-
bed roles looks out from his or her sometimes fragile haven,
the outsider in society gazes at the spectacle of people
gathered so profoundly into these tiny permanent groups.
The growing family is the institution in which one can see
and live through all the processes of order and stability,
conflict and change that are experienced less personally,
for the most part, in the rest of society.

Social policy and the welfare state have the family as one
of its major targets. Social workers are taught how to
support the family with all kinds of techniques from budget
management to family therapy. Teachers, doctors and
nurses are constantly aware of its significance in their work
with its members. Housing departments in local authorities
have until recently given priority to the housing of families.
Both the major political parties stress the family's fundamental importance. At the same time, the nuclear family
has over the last decade or so been subject to enormous and
deeply-felt criticism about its too powerful place in the lives
of us all and about the destructive possibilities of this small
endlessly momentous unit.

The family as a value or a set of values is particularly
difficult to think about, to be somewhat detached about,
because our personal involvement is deep as well as wide.
To become detached, one risks losing some of that depth,
which is one's own identity. To consider the values involved in the family it is peculiarly necessary to be able to
tolerate ambiguity, uncertainty, feeling as well as reason,
and a preparedness to be reflexive – to recognise that the
inside observer is as much a part of the process of observation as the phenomenon being observed.

THE FAMILY AND THE STATE

The family is one of the social institutions of society: the
state is a formal political construct within society, at some
periods of history rather marginal in its influence and, at
others, as at the present time, rather pervasive. The
legislation lying behind the welfare state tends to see the

family as the first line of support for most citizens in the
troubles of their lives and at their vulnerable periods –
childhood, old age, child-bearing; the state is seen as
residual, (4) supporting individuals when the family system
fails. Primary social responsibility is placed on the
nuclear family, and particularly on women.

The proportion of old people in the population has greatly
increased through this century – from 5 per cent over 65 in
1901 to 13 per cent in 1971, and that proportion is likely to
be nearer 20 per cent in the fairly near future; the proportion of people over 85 increased ninefold in that same
period. (5)   Most old people who cannot manage easily on
their own are cared for still within the family system. (6)
Virtually all rely on the old age pension, contributed
towards during the years of work, though actually paid for
out of present state income.   Out of the total money spent
every year by social services departments, one-third is
spent consistently on the maintenance of local authority old
people's homes.   In addition, the majority of the home-help
and nursing service resources, as well as a high proportion
of bed-spaces in hospitals, are employed in the specific care
of the old, in relation to the particular problems of being
old.

The other large and vulnerable age-group, children, is
also supported largely by the institution of the family, and in
fact mainly brought into society by this means.   At any one
time, children are the responsibility of a minority of households – three-quarters of all dependent children are living
in 22 per cent of UK households, and over half the dependent children are in fewer than 13 per cent of households. (7)   Thus child-bearing and child-rearing responsibilities are, at any one time, quite unevenly spread through
the population.   Many children do not live in the 'normal'
nuclear family; Finer (8) found in the early 1970s that of
the fourteen million children in the population, 920,000
lived with their mother as the sole parent, and 160,000
lived with their father.   This takes the number of children
in one-parent families to well over one million.   Also,
divorce decrees greatly affect the lives of children living in
nuclear families; there were 106,000 decrees in 1973, for
example, affecting 127,000 children, and the number rises
every year.   By the late 1970s the state was really heavily
involved in the basic care of children, with the number of
children in care topping 100,000 and rising overall and proportionately in relation to the child population every year.

The position of women in society is deeply influenced by
their unpaid responsibilities in the family. 'They live dis-
persed among the males attached through residence, housework, economic conditions and social standing to certain
men'. (9) This could also be said about the position of
children, except for the bit about housework. And the
more the state backs up the primacy of the nuclear family,
the more the social worker continues to encourage a mother
to cope with the vagaries of her particular lot, the more the
doctor encourages so many women patients to manage on
tranquillisers, so the state supports an institution that is
certainly in its own economic interest,as the family cares
for the majority of children and old people. The cost to the
pivot of the family, the mother, may however be enormous.
In Brown's and Harris's recent careful study of depression
in women, they report that out of the women they studied in
their main group, 'each woman in Camberwell had an average
of four "difficulties": and about half had one of sufficient
severity to cause, as far as we could judge, considerable
and often unremitting distress'. (10) Virtually all of these
difficulties were family based. 'The incidence of depression among women without children were less than half that
of working class women with children': (11) many of these
women had no adult confidant with whom to share their difficulties, as they tended to lose emotional intimacy with their
husbands when caring for children. (12)

The conflicts involved in the position of women become
even more morally disturbing when one considers the situation of the Asian girl, wife and mother. The paradox of all
families is given in this statement from Amrit Wilson's book
on the lives of Asian women, (13) but it is particularly
poignant for people whose whole sense of meaning, and self-
esteem, has been tied up with their families: 'my family is
like a part of myself, or my body; if I cut if off I could die.
But it is a part which gives me so much pain that sometimes
I can't bear it – can't bear it at all.' George Brown's work
on depression in women indicates that women of many nation-
alities suffer this same deep involvement. (14)

The importance of the family in society and the state also
bears on the low status given to people not living in families.
Twenty per cent of the population now live alone, 40 per cent
of old people do so. That so much of state provision is
geared to families and that single people are made to feel as
of less importance does matter, and is again related to the
strength of the nuclear family. Though it is an institution

that supports many loving relationships in society (and many
hostile ones), it is fundamentally exclusive. You are either
in it, with all its troubles, or out of it, with all the isolation. This is a fact known most deeply by children in care,
by old people without relatives, by Asian girls fleeing from
an arranged marriage, by single people seeking council
houses.
The functions of the family have been exhaustively analysed by functionalist sociologists. In a large, confusing,
alienating society, it is necessary for individuals to have a
'nest', somewhere relatively safe in which to relate intimately to others, to find a sense of personal identity, and to
produce and bring up children: (15)
    The modern American family is not ... facing dissolution
    but has become stripped down to two essential functions.
    Its most important function is that of the socialisation of
    the child. This is functional both for the individual per-
    sonalities of the children (and indeed the parents) and for
    society as a whole. But second, the modern family also
    performs the function of 'stabilisation of the adult person-
    alities of the population of society'. This is related to
    the central importance of marriage in our society and the
    way in which it is increasingly perceived in 'human rela-
    tions' terms. Thus higher divorce rates do not neces-
    sarily indicate a flight from the institution of marriage but
    may, paradoxically, reflect the higher expectations that
    individuals have of marital relations.
Berger and Kellner in a most interesting article describe the
life-long dialogue that two individuals can have in a marriage (or in any close relationship) that creates their sense
of reality jointly: 'a social arrangement that creates for the
individual the sort of order in which he can experience his
life as making sense ... the reality of the world is sustained through conversation with significant others.' (16)
Marriage is, in many ways, personally, in society and in
the state, a considerable factor in maintaining social order.
    The welfare state incorporates the nuclear family in its
legislation. Within the social security system, for
instance, it is the duty of the parent to support the child
financially and bring him or her up. Also it is the duty of a
man to support the woman he is living with, married or not,
as is demonstrated by the social security method of checking
on the living arrangements of single women living on their
allowances. There are some commensurate duties for
women towards their husbands. As the family is regarded

by the state as the main institutional means of supporting its
members, there is a danger that assistance to members will
weaken the system: 'Social security often walks the tight-
rope between its wishes to support the family and its fear
lest the help it provides undermines either the very family
virtues it wants to foster or other social values that over-
ride family considerations.' For example, 'separated and
divorced families, unlike widowed families, are generally
held partly responsible for their condition in addition to the
fact that their conduct is seen to be threatening to the institutions of marriage and the family.' (17)

National insurance and taxation are also very family-
based, being addressed to the husband and father in the
first instance, and related to a whole system of family
dependencies.

Within the education system, it is the duty of the parent
to see that the child is properly educated, and parents can
be prosecuted if they fail to carry out this function. In
educational research, there is an acknowledgment of the
fundamental influence the family has on the child, particularly during the first five years, but also throughout school.
The Plowden Committee of 1967 (18) laid great emphasis on
the power of the family: 'The National Survey points to the
influence upon educational performance of parental attitudes.
It follows that one of the essentials for educational advance
is a closer partnership between the two parties to every
child's education.' This is still one of the political battles
within the educational field. The Taylor Report (19) was
published recently on the relative position of educational and
parental forces in the governing of schools. There is a
clash here between the interests of professionals, bureaucrats and the family, and the result is very different from
the comparable American system, where parents exercise
much more direct power over curriculum as well as other
educational matters.

The family is regarded as highly important, too, in the
personal social services. This is nowhere so clear as in
the unmistakable tone of the 1960 Ingleby Report, (20) where
the controlling function of the family in society is beauti-
fully, if naively, laid out. It is worth-while quoting at
some length:

> The primary responsibility for bringing up children is
> parental and it is essentially a positive responsibility.
> It is the parents' duty to help their children to become
> effective law-abiding citizens by example and training and

by providing a stable and secure family background in
which they can develop satisfactorily.... Parents vary
in their capacity to live up to this ideal and children also
vary in the degree to which they are a problem to their
parents. Some families suffer misfortune, or are victims of difficult circumstances, others are just adequate.
... It is the duty of the community to provide through
its social and welfare services the advice and support
which such parents and children need; to build up their
capacity for responsibility and to enable them to fulfil
their proper role.

You couldn't get it much clearer than that!

The tone of the later, 1974, Finer Report is very different, but the importance of the family as a unit is still
stressed: (21)

The family is the basic institution which prescribes the
conditions for sexual relationships, childbearing and
child rearing, and ensures in the course of socialising
the young, the transmission of ethical and cultural values
across the generations. It is the unit within which most
men and women find themselves best able to satisfy not
only their sexual needs, but also the psychic needs of
sympathy, mutual aid and intimacy ... the first and dominant purpose of the law is to uphold the family.

This is not very different in meaning from the Ingleby
Report, after all, and a very functional view in a committee
convened to consider the needs of one-parent families.

In fact the general official support for the family from all
political parties is great enough for Ministries of the Family
to be seriously suggested. It is recognised that this support can cut across general economic trends. Margaret
Wynn has been a constant advocate of the financial needs of
the family, and has published a well-known book on family
policy. (22) She acknowledges the positive effort that is
required within the welfare state to safeguard the
family: (23)

family policy proposes to influence the evolution of economic forces away from what is adverse to the family to
what is beneficial to the family. Family policy proposes
the redistribution of national wealth and income in favour
of children, or, in other words, the transfer of resources
to investment in future generations. Economic forces
tend to develop adversely to the interests of families if
left to their own evolution: every country therefore needs
a family policy.

It is interesting that in this argument children are seen as economic assets, and the rationale is capitalist.

In some London boroughs, until very recently, housing has been family based. Families with children have priority. The standard unit has tended to be the three-bedroomed council house. It is only quite rarely that the state does not seem to see its task as related to the nuclear family unit. However, the National Health Service, for instance, makes its services available to everyone, regardless of family position or non-position. And there is a section in the Seebohm Report which addresses itself to its clientele: (24)

We decided very early in our discussions that it would be impossible to restrict our work solely to the needs of the two or even three generation families. We could only make sense of our task by considering also childless couples and individuals without any close relatives: in other words, everybody.

This has made for some confusion in many social services departments, as most legislation is family based and there is no over-riding instruction, as there is in Scotland, to consider the needs of the whole community; but in practice it means that people on their own and not coming into one of the legislative categories are not so readily refused help as they would have been in the past.

We can see then that the state and the family have a quite remarkable mutual interdependence, and it is only in the few fields of social policy that people are considered irrespective of their family position. During the last few years there has been a great wave of theoretical criticism of the nuclear family, arising both from the work of Laing, Cooper and Esterton (25) and from the women's liberation movement. Many workers in the welfare services have also been aware that many people do not bring up children within the conventional nuclear family system: the classic extended family pattern has been known about and studied since the beginnings of the welfare system, but the Asian and West Indian family structures now increase the complexity of the picture; many children, as has just been mentioned, grow up in one-parent families, or their families are affected by divorce and re-marriage; some children actually ask to be received into care.

VIEWS OF THE FAMILY

Of all the social institutions in this society, the family
attracts the most diverse views, from theorists and activists
alike.

The marriage relationship can be seen as the most significant one that most people have, the one that gives them most
meaning. But even this pair-bonding is culturally determined, and the urge to find 'one partner' can be seen as
much as a curse as a blessing. Children and older members of the family can be loved as individuals, and also seen
as representing continuity and evolution in a society that
usually changes rapidly and in - to most people - unforeseen
directions. A good family and good parenting can give individuals the inner strength and integrity on which they can
more easily build the rest of their lives.

But Laing, for instance, has criticised the alienation of
the person in society and the way this springs from bad faith
in the family: (26)

One of the most hellish whirligigs of our contemporary
interpersonal alienation is that of two alienated lovers,
two self-perpetuated solitudes, each in emptiness feeding
on the others emptiness, an inextricable and timeless confusion, tragic and comic - the everfertile soil of endless
recrimination and desolation.

Morgan describes the family as 'a constant assault on the
self; it is perhaps the most total of total institutions'. (27)
The mad family can represent a mad world. A family can
be a prison, as Hannah Gavron pointed out in the very title
of her book, 'The Captive Wife', and the subtitle 'Conflicts
of Housebound Mothers': the prison-like nature of much of
the mother's experience there is found fifteen years later in
Brown and Harris's recent book on depression in women
already quoted. (28) The house, the children and the role
can be not only a prison but a place of violence, too, as the
campaign in the 1970s for the recognition of battered wives
and the most recent growth of awareness of violence to
children proves. The home can be literally a place of
death as well as love. Two children a day die from attack
by their own parents. (29) To grow up in a loving family is
a good experience: to be at the mercy of two adults who are
either depressed, indifferent or sadistic is tragic. For a
child in a nuclear family has all his eggs in one basket: and
the most private the family is, the more he or she is likely
to reflect the characteristics of that living group. All bio-

graphies begin with the family of origin: it is from these
little groups that history is created.

But the family as we have it now is another manifestation
of the capitalist society. Ehrenreich and English demonstrate in their book on '150 years of the experts' advice to
women' (30) that the 'home' is a concept created as a contrast to the harsh world outside: 'the genteel lady of leisure
was as much a part of the industrial social order as her husband or his employees': (31) she, her sickness, hysteria,
frailty and dependence were a necessary part of the middle-
class scene. The home is a romantic vision. In John
Ruskin's view: (32)

> this is the true nature of home – it is the place of peace;
> the shelter, not only from all injury, but from all terror,
> doubt and division. In so far as it is not this, it is not
> home; so far as the anxieties of the outer life penetrate
> into it, and the inconsistently minded, unknown, unloved
> or hostile society of the outer world is allowed by either
> husband or wife to cross the threshold it ceases to be a
> home; it is then only part of the outer world which you
> have roofed over and lighted fire in. But so far as it is
> a sacred place, a vestal temple, a temple of the hearth
> watched over by household gods ... so far it vindicates
> the name and fulfils the praise of home.

Men, women and children, young and old, should find in the
home a refuge. But the conservative utopia pictured here,
which is probably part of every industrialised person's view
of home, ignores the contradictions of this society which
will be present in every institution. The home is the place
where we learn to give and to receive authority – and where
power is also strongly present; many seek liberation from
the authority of their original home, and seek to set up their
own authoritative system in a new one.

Inequalities are maintained through the nuclear family, of
class, of sex, of age, of racial and regional differences.
The very fact that the state pays so much attention to its
maintenance demonstrates how tied up it is in the capitalist
system – both the economic class system and the sexual
class system. Its influence is great because it is so
deep. (33)

> It is the family as much as the nation that transmits the
> explicit and implicit norms of social class. Thus the
> exponents of tradition fear disintegration of the family,
> and the champions of social justice may view its persis-
> tence as an insurmountable obstacle to equality at the
> starting line.

Equality as a value is irrelevant in the Freudian concept of the nuclear family: 'equality for him [Freud] is a desire to avoid conflicts over Papa's love and nothing more than that that.' (34)   We grow up in families that are already identified – and usually identify themselves – in class terms. And the prevailing theory of the family, one that has been so influential through most of the twentieth century, promotes hierarchy as a principle and perceives any other view of relationships as having profound pathological components. Here politics, tradition and psychoanalysis come close together to emphasise the naturalness of hierarchy, both of class and sex.   Poster has an interesting chapter on Freud's concept of the family.   He writes: (35)

in the last instance, the praxis (therapy) that derives from his theory will end up as an accommodation to the existing ruling powers, not only to the groups that dominate the economy and politics but also to the groups that are in dominant positions in those places where the psyche is constituted, in the family where the male rules the female and, most significantly, where parents dominate children.

We grow up already accepting a large measure of someone else's authority.

How pervasive the hierarchy of sex is is argued by Simmel: (36)

if we express the historic relation between the sexes crudely in terms of master and slave, it is part of the master's privilege not to have to think continuously of the fact that he is the master while the position of the slave carried with it the constant reminder of his being a slave. It cannot be overlooked that the woman forgets far less often the fact of being a woman than the man of being a man.

Among the ideas already mentioned in this section are ones that have been very influential in the last few years.   One of these is that it is impossible to separate overt power in society at large from people's private sense of identity. People growing up with strong authoritarian leanings in a hierarchical family – which at the same time may be warm and loving – will carry out the requirements of society in these respects.   Because they really believe in and respect the system, do not question it, then they will gladly accept the authority of others and, in turn, wield it themselves without problems.

This is what is meant by the often repeated phrase 'the personal is political'.   We have been taught so much to think that an inner life is so different from social or political life,

that some things are private and others public and that the
two must not be mixed, that discretion and confidentiality
are prime values, that we are led to believe there is a great
gap between private experience and public life. It is in the
family that we tend to learn to distinguish these values, but
it is in the family that these distinctions are the most unreal.
    The other important, very English, value is given in
Simmel's statement. A middle-class heterosexual white
man may never realise that he is powerful because he accepts
his life-position as being normal. He has to be exception-
ally imaginative to realise that other people's life experience
is really different from his own. This is nicely illustrated
in Edith Wharton's 'The Age of Innocence' published originally in 1920, when the fairly sensitive hero suddenly queries
why, in nineteenth-century New York respectable society,
women shouldn't have the same freedom as men. This question keeps on occurring to him through the novel, though the
way he actually leads his life is in the manner culturally
laid down for him. The point is that most people in that –
or probably in most – 'normal' societies never ask the question. The powerful don't have to realise they are powerful:
the essence of their strength is probably in the non-realisa-
tion, because then there is no reason for change. Because
family values are usually presented as normal values to their
children, it is the exceptional child who neither unthinkingly
accepts or – the opposite – totally rejects the values as presented and so, in either instance, remains tied up in the
system. It is working one's way through total acceptance
or total rejection to something of one's own that is the
essence of freedom: but people in this society are not encouraged to hold onto and to live with paradox and opposition, even though it surrounds them. The fact is that in the
family, as in any other institution, 'the terrible paradox,
that my freedom is bound up with your freedom' (37) cannot
be escaped. We need, to be relatively free, to live in
relation to other people and to the world around in all its
aspects, and yet to be ourselves. Family struggles to do
this are described in the 1970s Institute of Community
Studies' 'The Symmetrical Family'. (38)
    The family, in sociological and psychological studies, has
needed to be seen as non-political. It is now, however,
clear that the institution is deeply concerned with power.
Children, in order to become recognisable human beings,
have to be brought up in the family, usually the nuclear
family; and that very socialisation process is a powerful

transmission of personal and social values. There is no way to do it in a neutral manner. Psychoanalytic theory places virtually all the significant events there, in early childhood; humanistic psychology, more optimistically, emphasises growth and the many other important events in people's lives when they can change, become more or less themselves, understand and intelligently live with themselves and others. But the family is, of course, significant to us all.

If people are to believe they have some power and control, and if they are really to achieve this power, the movement towards participation involves the early institutions such as the family and the school. The 'training to subservience' can begin in the family, whether it is the children who are subservient, or the mother – or for that matter, the father or grandparents.

The family is also part of the split between the private and the public – the inward-looking nature of many families, the stress on the individual at the expense of the community. In this paradox, as in all the others, the family is both a product and a powerful influence on individuals, other social institutions and the structure and values of the society as a whole.

It is certainly in the family that we discern the relationship between history and biography, between the individual and society, between the forces of control and order and those of change. The family is supported by the state: it is an institution that is a vessel for some of our deepest feelings: it creates people, and all their potential for good and evil. The contradictions of the family are those which we feel about our whole existence.

5

Bureaucracy versus professionalism

The nature of authority over those processed through bureaucracies, and over the clients of professionals, is not identical. Both are significant, however.

'One of the outstanding features of twentieth century industrial society is the concentration of nearly all the working population into employment in bureaucratic organisations for a wage or salary'. (1) Ninety per cent of the employed population in Britain and the USA, no less, work in bureaucracies. (2) The professions are a minority of the employed, in contrast, but still a very characteristic and powerful phenomenon to us all. Both are linked to the scientific problem-solving method of thought and organisation so characteristic of Western society.

According to the level of analysis taken, the concepts of bureaucracy and professionalism can be taken as either potentially contradictory forces or distinguishable parts of the same system.

In one analysis, the contrast is between two distinct systems of getting things done. In the bureaucratic method, jobs too big for one person or a small group to do are organised into structures, which are typically hierarchical and work on the basis of carefully constructed rules, where the people involved are fitted into the slots already devised for them; it may be that no previous training is required. Professionalism and expertise, on the other hand, involve longer training and the internalisation of skills and values, so that the control already exists in people by the time they come to practise the job, and the need for external controls is minimal.

In the wider analysis, however, it can be seen that, in our present society, both the standard bureaucrat and the normal professional are part of the same social system which assumes the validity of hierarchy, whether he or she is functioning within a classified role or is practising an expertise which is deliberately kept as a mystery to everyone else, the laymen. Both methods of work are designed to combat uncertainty, and to bring order into structures and decision-making procedures. The running of modern organisations is a very complex matter, but its complexity is compounded by the secrecy, mystery and upward accountability of the structures in which we carry out this complexity.

The welfare state is largely administered through these two methods, within the representative mode of democracy.

BUREAUCRACY

Social scientists have been trying to understand the significance of bureaucracies since industrialisation, which on a large scale implies the accumulation of capital and, with this, the growth of huge organisations. Large commercial organisations employ people on a massive scale, in factories and offices, to develop the production, distribution and management of goods. Alongside, and following this growth in organisations commercially throughout the nineteenth and twentieth centuries, has been a commensurate development of the large state institutions for the administration of the laws relating to the citizens. Bureaucracies are the most obvious way of carrying out, routinely, large-scale tasks. Fundamental decision-making is concentrated in the top layers of the organisation, policies are filtered down through the machine. Information, more or less efficiently, comes upwards through the levels to assist in decision-making. Minor decisions are made at appropriate levels in the system, so that there is some controlled delegation of power. Managers become the essential mediators of action. Accountability, of course upwards, becomes the key virtue; you know whom to praise and whom to blame, at least internally. People become responsible to their superior rather than to their own definition of the task, or to their client. Policy comes downward. Efficiency becomes a primary virtue. Almost any organised task, beyond the very smallest and most informal, seems to have an inbuilt tendency to some characteristics of bureaucracy in its organisation; it is a most pervasive phenomenon.

Weber has offered a useful list of the characteristics of bureaucracy which has influenced almost all subsequent work. His seven classic factors are: 'a continuous organisation of official functions bound by rules'; hierarchy; a limited and specific area of competence for individuals; technical rules or norms administered by trained and experienced officials; employment in the agency to be separated from ownership of the agency; no right to the office by the incumbent; and the importance of written documents in the running of the agency. (3)

Studies of bureaucracy in this century have been of two entirely different kinds – managerial and sociological. The intention of the managerial work is to make bureaucracies work better. It is accepted that they exist, that the vast majority of people in an industrial state work in them, and the main problem is inefficiency. Managerial studies are usually prescriptive: what you ought to do to produce more work, more acceptable working conditions, a more coherent and rational power structure, better profits, better service.

The serious study of commercial organisations began in the United States in the 1920s with the work of F.W. Taylor, (4) has developed through the Organisation and Methods (O & M) stream, and is used freely both commercially and in local government at the present time: these methods are largely concerned with mechanistic efficiency. The Elton Mayo/Hawthorne School of the 1930s has developed the more humanistic side of managerial studies, though the end is the same – how to make better profits. These pieces of work take people and their happiness much more seriously into account, and in fact take work satisfaction as an important component of manufacture. Management theories have multiplied in the last decades, to the humanistic, questioning school of Argyris, to the justification of hierarchy related to different personal capacities of Jaques, to the popular development of rational decision-making theories of Management by Objectives and Programming, Planning, Budgeting Services (PPBS) which have greatly influenced local government organisation in this country. The reorganisation of the health service was carried out in 1974 under the aegis of management theories which many people now criticise. Maud and Mallaby (5) inevitably turned to management theorists in their deliberations about the future of local government. We are all influenced by their work and their assumptions whether or not we ourselves work in a hierarchy.

The extent of the influence of management theorists in the
welfare state, more particularly in local government, is
deeply criticised by two recent books, 'The Local State' by
Cynthia Cockburn and 'Local Government Becomes Big Business' by John Benington. In criticising management techniques, such studies as these become wider in their analysis, linking organisations to social structure in general,
and so are more sociological in their approach.
Benington gives figures to demonstrate the growth of
local authorities in the last half century. Public expenditure over the years 1919-70 has grown from one-sixth to
over half of the gross national product (GNP). Local government expenditure is now one-third of all public expenditure. To illustrate this disproportionate growth in local
government compared with other sections, he indicates that
during the 1960s GNP increased by 80 per cent, total expenditure by 120 per cent and local government expenditure by
170 per cent. (6) Local government now employs 10 per
cent of the total working population. Cockburn's material
on Lambeth further brings out the implications of this growth.
During the years 1967-74 the number of manual staff on Lambeth's payroll stayed constant at 3,600 while the number of
office staff doubled from 1,800 to 3,600. The council's
expenditure rose from £7.2m to £17.4m in the same period,
which was a 50 per cent growth even allowing fro inflation:
the council's indebtedness trebled from £39m to £114m, with
half the total income being used in paying back moneylenders
(including building societies) for loans.
Along with this enormous growth and indebtedness to the
market economy now being curtailed by the 1979 Conservative Government has come reorganisation, where management theories have become greatly important. (7)
In 1969-70 of all County Councils, only 47% had an overall
policy committee, 81% had a top level manager and 44% had
a management team. In 1973 every one of the new councils had all three.... Corporate management is now a
fact of life in local government.
One overriding tendency of management thinking is to con-
vert moral issues into technical issues: the fundamental
tendency of all bureaucratic thought is to turn all problems
of politics into problems of administration. (8) The principles of big business, particularly concerning profit and
loss, become increasingly significant. In Lambeth, (9)
the balance of authority and the nature of council decision-
making had changed quite strikingly. What had existed as

a loose assembly of council committees and a multiplicity
of small departments, their work barely co-ordinated,
had become a tightly knit hierarchy under the control of
a powerful board of directors, in close partnership with
a top-level caucus of majority party members [involved in
analytic planning].
The importance of the pyramid shape is the assumption
that important decisions are made at the top; within the
pyramid is a strong development of professional empires in
local government. As Benington writes, we can forget the
old cosy images of the town hall; the council can be seen
'less as a body of elected representatives, than as the
Board of Directors of a large investment corporation'.
This implies a 'view of politicians as financial managers who
are only loosely accountable to their shareholders.'
    Welfare state bureaucracies do not only have a tendency to
take on the form of commercialism: they are heavily involved with the commercial firms themselves. Cockburn describes these tentacles. For one thing, keeping the peace
in society and avoiding conflict at all costs is good for business, so this is particularly influential as a policy in local
government: this tends to lead to greater secrecy. A
second strand is the implications and obligations of heavy
loans made by the council: she comments on (10)
    the shareholders and directors of commercial firms in the
    City of Westminster that employ Lambeth's commuters, the
    finance companies in the City of London and abroad from
    whom the Council borrows a fair proportion of its massive
    loan, and whose operations lie behind so many movements
    of capital in the borough.
The final tie-up is that local government is a massive
employer in its own right £1,500m per annum is spent on
construction of buildings, and the local government system
supports 60 per cent of the construction industry and 90 per
cent of civil engineering. In all these areas - policy, employment and obligations to lenders - local government is an
intrinsic powerful part of the local capitalist system.
    It is easy to see how the local authority, with all these
threads, becomes dependent on the forces of commercialism
in the principles upon which it forms its policies. And the
interests of the City and big business may very well not be
the same as those of the ratepayers of a particular borough
- and are certain indeed not to be identical with the interests of the clients of a social services department. The
massive strength and weakness of bureaucracy is that

accountability is always upwards: it means in this instance that where there is a clash of interest between the individual protestor and the industrial forces that are both strongly influential and powerful in the system, the individual may stand less chance of personal attention than he did in the less 'managed' department of the past. Moreover, the town hall may now be so influenced by commercial forces that it is difficult to know how to reconcile their interests with those of the citizens receiving the services.

Such then are the management studies of bureaucracies, their growth, power and some of their critics. The other kinds of studies have been sociological, where the explicit analysis - like that of the critics of the management movement just discussed - is of the place and significance of bureaucracies in society. The intention here is not prescription but analysis: the attempt is to understand major institutions in society better and critically, not to make them work better. The analysis of bureaucracies is always part of a larger whole.

Weber's analysis, as already discussed, was part of his attempt to understand the control system of modern societies, and the different bases of authority. Marx's view was part of his class analysis of society. The American modern theorists such as Wright Mills, Parsons, Gouldner, Goffman and Etzioni have all written on the nature of bureaucracy, each with his particular understanding of its significance.

It is impossible, out of the vast amount of sociological literature on bureaucracy, to summarise the different perspectives and analyses. I would just like to comment on the workings of bureaucracy by quoting from the two major, but very different, figures who have discerned a major and seemingly universal characteristic, that of official secrecy. Marx saw state and industrial bureaucracies as the ready-made tool of the class in power: (11)

the bureaucracy has in its possession the affairs of State, the spiritual being of society; it belongs to it as a private property. The general spirit of bureaucracy is the official secret, the mystery.... Conducting the affairs of State in public, even political consciousness, these appear to the bureaucracy as high treason against the mystery. Authority is thus the principle of its knowledge, and the deification of authoritarianism is its credo. But within itself this spiritualism turns into a coarse materialism, the materialism of dumb obedience.... As

far as the individual bureaucrat is concerned, the goals
of the State become his private goals: a hunting for higher
jobs and the making of a career.... Bureaucracy has
thus to make life as materialistic as possible. The
bureaucrat sees the world as a mere object to be managed
by him.

This statement certainly rings true of the Britain of the
1970s, well over a hundred years after it was written.
Weber, fifty years after Marx, and writing from a very different perspective, puts forward similar analysis and
warning: (12)

Bureaucratic administration means fundamentally the
exercise of control on the basis of knowledge. This is
the feature that makes it specifically rational. This consists on the one hand in technical knowledge which, by
itself, is sufficient to ensure it a position of extraordi-
nary power. But in addition to this, bureaucratic organisations, or the holders of power who make use of them,
have the tendency to increase their power still further by
the knowledge growing out of experience in that service.
For they acquire through the conduct of office a special
knowledge of facts and have available a store of documen-
tary material peculiar to themselves. While not peculiar
to bureaucratic organisations, the concept of 'official
secrets' is certainly typical of them. It stands in relation to technical knowledge in somewhat the same position
as commercial secrets do to technological training.

The sociological analysis is of an outsider looking in, particularly at the power of dominant groups; the managerial
perspective is of a man making the system (of which he is a
part) work.

PROFESSIONALISM

The characteristics of professionalism, that other organisation of expertise, have also been enumerated by various
writers. Greenwood (13) gives the list: a body of skills
and knowledge; a prolonged period of training to acquire
these; acceptance of the validity of these skills by society
at large and therefore the exclusive right to practise them;
a professional culture and a code of ethics organised by
members of the profession. Also, since professionals
require education and considerable literacy, and since they
typically press for status and high income, they are a signi-

ficant factor in the class system. This means that the professionals too may represent the dominant culture in any
society - what it is appropriate to do, as opposed to, or as
well as, what is true. The professional can no longer be
completely disinterested once he has a stake in the society.
As Johnson points out in his 1977 version of 'Professions
and Power', 'professionalism is a successful ideology'. (14)

According to some accounts, some groups are without
doubt, 'full' professions - doctors, lawyers, architects,
university teachers. Others have been designated, by
sociologists rather than themselves, semi-professions -
teachers, social workers, nurses. Amitai Etzioni gives
the rationale for this: (15)

for certain purposes it is useful to distinguish between
those organisations employing professionals whose professional training is long (five years or more) and those
employing professionals whose training is shorter (less
than five years). The former we call fully-fledged professional organisations, the latter semi-professionals....
Pure professional organisations are primarily devoted to
the creation and application of knowledge; their professionals are usually protected in their work by the guaran-
tee of privileged communication, and they are often concerned with the communication, and, to a lesser extent,
the application of knowledge, their professionals are less
likely to be guaranteed the right of privileged communica-
tions, and they are rarely concerned with matters of life
and death.

(Though as a rider, that last observation does not seem to
apply to social workers, who may be working with parents
who are potential batterers of their children, or making
difficult decisions about old people living alone. Neither
does it apply to nurses.)

It is clear that professionalism, as bureaucracy, is about
meritocracy. Professionalism is also about order, with a
heavy emphasis on the long period of socialisation in which
the potential professional absorbs the norms and values of
the profession. As there is this long period of learning to
accept the role, the professional does not have to be bound
by bureaucratic rules to do his job. He has, hopefully,
already absorbed the message.

That professionalisation of any activity gives it more
clout in the present social system is pointed out by Kogan
within the educational fields: (16)

teachers' feelings about their place in society have

changed as have those of all hitherto submissive groups.
They have a livelier sense of their own position as salary
earners: their leaders now hob-nob with the general
trade union leaders. They find themselves facing a
wider set of issues deriving from changes in social and
economic values.... Teachers' associations have moved
from policies that are institutionally continuous to far
more disfunctive and tempestuous issues of social distribution and control. They still remain believers in the
continuities but these general movements put different
pressure on them which in turn affect their own methods
of putting on pressures.

But professionals themselves, in considering their structural position in society, go further than merely changing
their style; many also question their own basis of power
and the grounds on which it rests. Frankl wrote ten years
ago of America: (17)

the present situation seems to me different from any we
have known before because the professions themselves
have come to harbour a growing number of people whose
sympathy for the new social movements that are underway ha
has led them to perceive the professions to which they
belong as instruments of unresponsive conservatism.

Many of the most potent arguments against the professionalisation of services are drawn together in Illich's book,
'Disabling Professions', published in 1977. These articles
emphasise the way professional groups have cornered the
market of care and so infantilised the rest of us. Doctors
do not encourage us to have knowledge of our own bodies,
lawyers protect their monopoly of legal services, and university teachers hold on to their tenure and their favourable
conditions of work, often putting research and publication
before teaching. All depend on the needs of others; social
workers need poverty and emotional problems to exist in
others, dentists need bad teeth. All need to define their
knowledge as mysterious, expert and technical: (18)

Professionalised services communicate a world view that
defines our lives and our societies as a series of technical problems. This technical definition is masked by
symbols of care and love that obscure the economic interests of the servicers and the disabling characteristics of
their practices.

The disabling consists of seeing need as a deficiency in the
'client', and splitting this deficiency into specialised areas
to be served by separate professional groups.

A further dimension in analysis is in Ehrenreich and
English's study 'For Her Own Good', which is the power of
the masculine profession over women, an example of how the
dominant culture is imposed by professionals because all the
people concerned believe in the values advocated: (19)
   The relationship between women and experts was not
   unlike conventional relationships between women and men.
   The experts wooed their female constituency, promising
   the 'right' and scientific way to live, and women respon-
   ded - most eagerly in the upper and middle classes, more
   slowly among the poor - with dependency and trust.
Professionalism can iron over uncertainty through routine
in a similar way to the bureaucratic method: 'skill in
routine professionalism is the application of technique to
problems where the nature of the problem is assumed': (20)
routine can arm the professional against the 'moral
abyss' (21) of many of the problems which he or she has to
face: (22)
   Political and moral controversy also cramps the professional's style, and he will often excuse himself from en-
   gaging in their controversy on the grounds that he is a
   'professional' - a neutral, technical specialist whose task
   is to get on with the job in hand.
That this alienating process does not always happen to
professionals (nor presumably always to bureaucrats) is
shown in John Berger's beautiful study of a general prac-
titioner, 'A Fortunate Man', where the doctor studied is
both concerned for quality and confident and humble enough
to accept uncertainty.   Berger quotes him as saying: (23)
   you never know for certain about anything.   This sounds
   falsely modest and trite, but it's the honest truth.   Most
   of the time you are right and do appear to know but every
   now and then the rules seem to get broken and then you
   realise how lucky you have been on the occasions when
   you think you have known and been proved correct.
The author comments about the doctor: 'he never stops
speculating, testing, comparing.   The more open the question the more in interests him.'   This is the best of professionalism, nothing to do with status, class or privilege.
It is a professionalism that relates to rather than defends
against humanity.   Professionalism is often disabling to
others, but it need not be.   It is perhaps significant that
Berger's doctor worked alone, on his own responsibility.

THE AUTHORITY OF BUREAUCRATIC AND PROFESSIONAL ORGANISATIONS WITHIN THE WELFARE STATE

Bureaucracies, then, carry rational-legal authority, and professionals that of expertise, in today's society. We can see the different institutions in the welfare state as having differing bases of authority. A hospital, for instance, is largely a bureaucratic structure with a strong administrative hierarchical format, but this is modified by the very important status of the most powerful professional group, the doctors. Since Salmon, (24) nurses are now in the interesting position of a semi-profession organised in a bureaucratic structure. Doctors, on the other hand, being a far stronger, better paid profession, and of course largely masculine, work in 'firms' with a chief professional, a consultant, as head. The National Health Service has been bureaucratised further by the 1974 reorganisation, and there have also been attempts to delegate decision-making through the different levels and with the creation of Community Health Councils (CHCs). Patients are certainly at the bottom of the hierarchy (if one can even count them in the system at all, except as recipients), though there are now far more pressure groups and some CHCs seem remarkably effective, considering their technically impotent position.

Similarly, a school, though an organisation consisting entirely of professionals or semi-professionals and their pupils, is arranged as a pyramid, with considerable power and the possibility of charismatic authority belonging to the head. Individual teachers in theory are paramount in their own classrooms, but many studies indicate the strength of the school ethos and structures; it is difficult for any teacher to work in a way significantly different from that of his colleagues. Pupils again are at the bottom or maybe are the recipients. The power of the teachers' unions is increasing, and it is interesting to see that some pupils are now emulating this method of organisation and are appearing with petitions at teachers' union conferences. The authority of teachers is enhanced and maintained by the definition of knowledge present in many schools and which, as Young has indicated, (25) maintains the educational and the class hierarchy: it is the teachers' definition of knowledge which is considered important, not the pupils'.

Social services departments are bureaucratic rational-legal agencies, conducted for the most part with a social

work style. Social workers are in fact a minority of those
employed - one-eighth of each department approximately -
and only half of these are trained. One of the few
analytic articles on social work, that by Joel Handler,
stated: (26)

> it is time for children's officers - and other social
> workers - to reconsider their psychiatrist-client rela-
> tionship with those they seek to help. They are adminis-
> trative officials exercising governmental powers.

It is interesting to see how social workers have been
trained to accept the prevailing authority. In R.A. Scott's
study - Professional Employees in a Bureaucratic Structure
- he explains: (27)

> disciplined conformity to authority was regarded as a
> sign of maturity. As one supervisor explained to a re-
> calcitrant worker, 'Maturity is involved in working with
> existing authority and accepting it'. Another phrase
> often used to justify working within agency policy was that
> to do so was to 'accept the reality factors in the situa-
> tion.' To resist agency policy was considered unrealis-
> tic and a waste of energies which could be devoted to con-
> structive work.

Deacon and Bartley's study finds similar characteristics:
'the avoidance of the analysis of structures, the emphasis
on individuals, all make it an admirable set of ideas for
somebody not wishing to disturb the status quo'. (28)   Other
writers question the bureaucratic authority and advocate
professionalism.   Glastonbury, in arguing that the social
service departments have too easily accepted the local government structure (a criticism I heartily agree with),
writes (29)

> I am arguing that for its effective operation the social
> service department as a front line organisation, needs a
> concentration of authority and resources at the point
> where the work is being done: this offers a pragmatic
> case for the recognition of professional autonomy in
> social work, and questions the utility of an administrative
> hierarchy.

A consideration of the authority of professionalism and,
even more strongly, bureaucracy brings into focus many of
our deepest fears about the world we are living in, and, as
employees of the welfare services, helping to maintain.
This is 'the brave new world of the technocrat, the hierarchy of alpha/beta/gamma people and the all-pervasive
managers' that Huxley so much feared, the '1984' which is

approaching so rapidly, the mysterious world of Kafka's nightmares. It is in this sense that bureaucracy and pro-fessionalism are partners in the same system, even though in everyday life they often seem to represent contrary values. Bureaucracies are admirable for routinised work; professionalism promotes new knowledge and, on the whole, efficiently organises the technical field of concern. But the authority we give to these structures too easily belittles the people who are the recipients of these services. The price of relative freedom from these forces, if it is possible at all in this society, is certainly constant vigilance. The uncertainties and moral problems of our lives cannot be routinised, scientifically ordered and solved technically. Where powerful structures, useful and orderly, hide the personal moral responsibility of individuals, then these organisations become dangerous for people's individual and collective freedom.

6

DECISION-MAKING: RATIONALITY VERSUS NEGOTIATION

We live in a society and a state where the typical formal
systems are bureaucratic and to a much lesser degree expert
and professional, governed largely by a representative
system with a few stabs at participation, and where the
basic economic dynamic of scarce resources and infinite
need is reasonably obvious. The society is fundamentally
capitalist; the state makes welfare provisions through a
vast panoply of legislation. The whole is a series of compromises between opposing systems and contradictory
values.

How do we make decisions in this society? This chapter
is about theories of decision-making related to administrative practice. The theories have been developed at different times in the twentieth century, and are themselves based
on a picture of the essential nature of man in society, and
particularly man in organisations. Views on this have
changed from the picture of 'economic man' in the nineteenth
and earlier part of the twentieth century, through a picture
of 'administrative man' (a product of the management theorists of the mid-twentieth century) to the most recent sociological theories of the social construction of reality – man
as the constant negotiator of his world.

Decision-making often seems a key to the contradictory
forces which is the subject of these essays; it is in making
decisions that the compromises have, if possible, to be
reached, the ideas and the feelings that the participants
bring have to be forged – hopefully – into a single unity, and
the structural forces involved simplified in a single action or
forced into conflict because compromise is not feasible.
Decision-making sums up the predominant activity of many
administrators, politicians and professionals. It is

remarkable how little attention practitioners pay to this most significant skill and process. It is in making decisions that the forces of reason and power meet.

The classic theories are those of rationality. Rational man is economic man: he maximises profit and looks after his own interest; his actions, combined with the actions of all other economic beings, work together for the common good. The system is the market system. The demand/ supply dynamic, based on the self-interest of all, works in the interest of all. Weber, (1) writing at the turn of the century, used rationality as the basis of one of his types of authority: rational-legal authority is impersonal, it works on known rules, and man is supposed to be a thinker, not a being who also feels.

The theory of rational decision-making is very specific. It defines the area of conflict. Lindblom asked: 'how far can we go in reasoning out policy instead of fighting over it?' and answers his question - and ours - when he writes: (2)

a good way to find out is to specify what a man has to do to analyse a problem rationally, and see where he runs into difficulties. A 'classical' formulation runs like this:-

i) faced with a given problem;

ii) a rational man first clarifies his goals, values and objectives, and then ranks or otherwise organises them in his mind;

iii) he then lists all important possible ways of - policies for - achieving his goals

iv) and investigates all the important consequences that would follow from each of the alternative policies;

v) at which point he is in a position to compare consequences of each policy with goals

vi) and so choose the policy with consequences most closely matching his goals.

The activity most consistent with this approach is playing a game like chess - an activity which is usually carried out in a cool and rational atmosphere, and where the object is clear - to win.

Why is it that our decision-making activities seem far away - or at least significantly unlike - this picture?

Herbert Simon points out that assumptions about man's nature are most precise in this model: (3)

economic man has a complete and consistent system of preferences that allows him always to choose between the

choices open to him; he is always completely aware of
what these alternatives are; there are no limits on the
complexity of the computations he can perform in order to
determine which alternatives are best; probability calcu-
lations are neither mysterious nor frightening to him.
We can immediately begin to see what is unsatisfactory about
the pure rationality principle, as economic man bears little
relation to the politicians, administrators and professionals
that we see around us, in the welfare state and elsewhere.
But rational decision-making is also clearly aimed at by
many people having to take delicate and difficult decisions,
in attempts to predict such as Management by Objectives and
the group of systems based on Programme, Planning,
Budgeting Services, and in the careful working out of action
practised by many individuals and organisations.

In order to see the principle of rationality clearly, we
have to think about some of its limits:

... 'faced with a given problem'. Among the people faced
with a decision, there may be little agreement what 'the
problem' is. What is more, the participants may not realise
the extent of their disagreement because it is fairly rare for
people to be entirely clear about their own assumptions and
stereotypes. This is one of the major problems in participatory decision-making, where there is less structure for
recognising conflict. Also, a group of people may even
have different languages in which to discuss the issues
before them.

Mayer and Timms (4) brought this out clearly in their
study of perceptions of social work by the social worker on
the one hand and the 'client' on the other. Cicourel (5)
demonstrated the language difference between police and
probation officers in labelling the same people 'sick' on the
one hand or 'criminal' on the other; these labels were, as
is the case with so many of the labels employed in the
'people-processing' organisations in the welfare state,
utilised as a diagnosis, and followed by a series of consequences. It is very clear in the Cicourel study that the
person, the subject of the action, is a sheet upon which a
whole variety of assumptions, diagnoses and remedies can
be printed. And the people taking the actions, from within
the framework in which they have come to operate, 'see'
the person in the way they do, as 'really' sick or criminal
or deprived, and find it difficult to conceive that the subject
himself, or a person with another way of thinking, could
see the problem in any other way. Class differences in

the way people see the world and the language they have to describe it in have been analysed both by Bernstein and by his critics, (6) but the framework from which we all think and feel is influenced not only by class but by cultural, professional, racial, sexual and many other different social forces.

In questioning the common-sense definition of 'what the problem is', by considering the consciousness that people bring to any decision-making activity, we are using the development of the particular branch of the sociology of knowledge labelled ethnomethodology, the clearest definition of which is set out in Berger's and Luckmann's book published just over ten years ago, 'The Social Construction of Reality'. Bernstein, Cicourel, and Mayer and Timms, already quoted, are all influenced by the same system of thinking exemplified in that book. Berger and Luckmann, in explaining the fundamental tenets, write 'everyday life presents itself as a reality interpreted by men and subjectively meaningful to them as a coherent world'. (7) But each person's inner world is different. We each take our own world around with us and, when asked to think about a certain problem, have only this world to bring.

The disjuncture caused by the different worlds existing in decision-making scenarios can be seen in committees and groupings everywhere; between a politician and a civil servant, (8) maybe a doctor and a patient, a teacher and a pupil, a social worker and a 'client'. In many case conferences brought together to make vital decisions about, say, a child's life, many different languages and ways of thinking/value systems may be present – including, sometimes, now, that of the child and his parent. Whatever the process is in making the definition of the problem, it is usually decidedly different from rationality in the classical sense of the term. In all the people present, there may be real differences, too, in aims and interests, a conflict rather than a consensus situation. But certainly perceptions of 'the problem' may well be many and varied.

... 'clarifies his goals'. The goals an individual has when working within the state machinery may be not only his own. An administrative man is typically working within, and representing, an organisation. Large organisations are complex, contain many different layers of thinking and perhaps many goals, some at least potentially in conflict with one another. A person's role within an organisation is likely to affect his other thinking: 'within organisations especially of the complex type, there is a technique of decision, an organisational process of thinking, which may not be analogous to that of the individual.' (9)

Over the last twenty years or so, in sociology, there have been many studies of the effect of organisations on individuals and on the processes, including decision-taking, happening within them. Many studies have paid particular attention to power maintenance within organisations, especially the power struggles involved when there are conflicts of values - for instance, 'Warwick University Ltd', (10) a study of commercial values in an academic institution, or 'Asylums', (11) the well-known book on the 'underlife' of closed institutions. The work done by Terry and Pauline Morris (12) on one prison system, Pentonville, is an analysis of layers within the prison, and the diversity of values and structures within one organisation; Lambert published a study of boarding schools, (13) and described the different lives, and layers of lives, contained within the same fabric, as Pauline Morris has done more recently about children's hospitals, 'Put Away'. Burns and Stalker offer a distinct kind of analysis of organisational complexity in their study of the forces that make for the carrying out of stable tasks in organisations, and those which encourage creativity, 'The Management of Innovation'. All these are classic studies of organisational diversity and their effects upon the people working within them. A man, or woman, responsible with others in the making of decisions, is typically not representing himself or herself alone, but is taking part in a far more complex scene, acting in an organisational role.

... 'Lists all the important possible ways of - policies for - achieving his goals'. Thinking out alternatives is often considerably limited in the welfare state by four main factors: the shortage of resources which often determine provision - for example, we found in a study in decision-making in Children's Departments (14) that the first question often asked, when there was an application for reception into care, was about the possibility of residential home vacancies; second, that administrators are often working in a situation of considerable uncertainty about the influence of complex factors; (15) third, the constraints of the general social values to which most people subscribe; and finally, that people tend to work on precedence - they do what they did before. In most jobs involving a certain amount of routine it is relatively rare for people to work out issues and their possible consequences from first principles.

Also, in administrative decision-making, routine tends to take over from an acute and constant awareness of ends and goals. This applies also to the last criterion I would like to comment on.

... 'investigates possible consequences'. Once again, in a routinised work-place, there will be many 'hidden agendas', vested interests, already-worked-out codes, that will influence the course of most decisions. This applies to expert decisions by professionals, more particularly those working in organisations, who have developed a style of individual working over a long period. Sometimes, too, decisions involve prediction, and a thrust towards effectiveness – for instance, the contract work that is now being used by some social workers (16) or the methods taken by a doctor to mend a broken body; but all too often alternative consequences which would follow different actions are calculated only vaguely if at all. Often work within the welfare state is done for the exercise of skill (as is often the case in social work) or for the accomplishment of administrative and legal tasks, rather than primarily for a specific end, at least in the mind of the person carrying out the task. Institutionalised fulfilment of tasks is the primary raison d'etre of a bureaucracy; to accomplish the due process is its strength and its weakness.

In practice, then, it is clear that the rationality model does not accord with the actual activity in the welfare state. People work in systems, carry preconceptions and assumptions around with them, are swayed by often contradictory considerations, work often in conflict rather than consensus situations, speak different languages. Our first model of decision-making has many limitations: economic man in the classic sense may exist, but he is rarely if ever met in working life.

Herbert Simon, writing in the 1940s, in fact presents the concept of 'limited rationality' to meet these criticisms. He states: (17)

> to anyone who has observed administrative organisations, or has concerned himself with their theory, it seems obvious enough that human behavior in organisations is, if not wholly rational, at least in part, intendedly so ... it is precisely in the realm where human behavior is intendedly rational, but only limitedly so, that there is room for a genuine theory of organisation and administration.
> ... Administrative theory is peculiarly the theory of intended and bounded rationality – of the behavior of

human beings who <u>satisfice</u> because they have not the wits
to <u>maximise</u>.... Administrative man recognises that the
world he perceives is a drastically simplified model of the
buzzing, blooming confusion that constitutes the real
world.

Simon's book, 'Administrative Behavior', is a study wrought
from long years of experience in, and study of, administrative organisations. Simon is a management theorist, and
was, with other empirical investigators such as Elton Mayo
in the Hawthorne experiments of the 1930s, (18) one of the
workers first questioning the classic rational stance. We
strive towards reason according to our own view of the
world in the decisions that we make, but the results from
such diverse men as Hitler, Churchill and Stalin, or alter-
natively a trade union leader, an employer and a member of
the Cabinet, would clearly be very different from each other.
And we do not have to relate the theories to such august –
or, at least well known – people: a study of the decision-
making in any children's home, Area Health Authority or
housing department will do.

Simon used the classical model as his starting-point. In
the 1960s, however, Braybrooke and Lindblom, a philosopher
and an organisation theorist, set up an alternative proposi-
tion in their book, 'A Strategy of Decision': (19)

When a man sets out to solve a problem he embarks on a
course of mental activity more circuitous, more complex,
more subtle and perhaps more idiocyncratic than he perceives. If he is aware of some of the grosser aspects of
his problem solving, as when he consciously focusses his
attention on what he identifies as a critical unknown, he
will often have only the feeblest insight into how his mind
finds, creates, dredges up – which of them he does not
know – a new idea. Dodging in and out of the unconscious, moving back and forth from concrete to abstract,
trying chance here and system there, soaring, jumping,
backtracking, crawling, sometimes freezing on a point
like a bird dog, he exploits unusual processes that are
only slowly yielding to observation and systematic description.

This really nice quotation is about creativity as well as
rationality in decision-making. It is about discovering the
new thing, as well as getting on with the old as efficiently
as possible.

Their book puts forward an alternative to rationality
models under the rather startling heading of 'disjointed

incrementalism'. Braybrooke and Lindblom believe that we tend to take decisions on the basis of past actions, on precedent, but modify each fresh decision marginally because of the exigencies of the present situation: in other words, decisions are made on the basis of the past with incremental changes. Because similar social movements tend to be taking place in different parts of a society at the same time, the incremental changes will tend to be similar in different places but will be 'disjointed', in fact, because they are not co-ordinated. This is also, of course, a theory of evolutionary social change. And principles spring from action rather than the other way round – an inductive model rather than the deductive, starting-from-first-principles paradigm used as the basis of the rationality idea.

The idea of disjointed incrementalism can be seen at its clearest in case law, in the system of law. The authors quote the principle of 'ex factor ius oritor' – 'the law springs from the fact'; in other words, cases should be decided on their own merits, based on past principles and practice, but taking into account the actual circumstances of the particular case. The authors quote from Radbruch (20) that this system of decision

> should be taken to signify that the concrete necessity of deciding a genuine case has considerably more interest for the creative energies of judges than the phantoms of imaginary cases can, floating about in the mind of a codifier who is trying to formulate a chief principle of law ... the jurist does not want to become insensitive through preconceived ideas to the lessons of an infinitely changeable and unforeseeable course of future experience.

Once again, there is a notion that decision-making is about people deriving satisfaction from practising their own skills, particularly when the effect of an action is in doubt.

The inductive style of decision-making was the predominant style among the social workers that we studied in working with children. (21) It is Kogan's view (22) that change in education often comes from practice, which is then later converted into principle. In other words, change can come from the bottom upwards, by practice, as well as from the top downwards, by principle. This view has its corollary in some recent theoretical sociological work – for instance, Glaser's and Strauss's 'The Discovery of Grounded Theory', which is concerned with the development of knowledge rather than the making of administrative decisions, but which similarly lays emphasis on the activity springing from experience and leading to principles, rather than the other way round.

The question of order and change is the mainspring of the
final set of theories on decision-making that I want to men-
tion. During the 1960s sociologists were working on the
idea of the social construction of reality (23) - how any
human being attempts to make sense in his world, and nego-
tiates his way through it. An article by Strauss and his
colleagues (24) is specifically on the American health service - The Hospital and its Negotiated Order. The discussion here is about how rules, decisions and ways of working
are negotiated in practice: 'hospital rules seem to us fre-
quently less explicit than tacit, probably as much breached
and stretched as honoured'. (25) Here the emphasis in
decision-taking is on discretion, and on the use of the system
by those participating in it; a long way away from rationality, unless one could argue that individual reason is taking
place at odds with the organisation - that the organisation is
being used in so far as it suits the individual.

Strauss and his colleagues discuss the factors already
mentioned as the limits to rationality - the influence of individual perception and stereotyping, the use of power, the
problem of medical and administrative uncertainty. Power
is more explicitly recognised than in any of the previous
theories. The relative power of the individuals or groups
concerned, rather than rationality, becomes the main dynamic. Instead of assuming value-consensus among the participants, they assume that conflict is basic; 'there is a
patterned variability of negotiation in the hospital' (26)
about who contacts whom, and about what, and what agree-
ments are made about medical and administrative issues.
Power is held by people with high status, particularly as
conferred by the most prestigious professions, and by those
with highly regarded values and skills. You have more
power if you have been in hospital for a longer period and
have therefore built up links and knowledge of resources.

This theory puts forward a scheme of negotiation and contract, mostly implicit, between people in getting work done.
Hidden agendas are taken for granted: whoever can impose
his meaning has power.

These then are the three major kinds of decision-making
theory, taking into account rationality, incrementalism and
power. In thinking about making decisions in this complex
institutionalised and conflicted society, we also need to pay
attention to the varieties of institutions and individuals
involved. The following factors are of importance:
    (a) the complexity of the situation in which the decision is

being made; whether an individual is making his own decisions, responsible to himself alone; whether a pair or
group is involved and the relationships between the parties,
including the power situation and the unconscious processes
in any group; the implications of working in any organisation, and the position of the individual within it; and finally
the constraints put on decisions by local or national
interests;

    (b) the particular framework, perceptions and values that
any individual brings, and whether he/she is aware of these;

    (c) the pressure in the style of decision-making towards
rationality and the consideration of first principles;

    (d) the economic constraints of decision;making;

    (e) the uncertainty that can be sustained in evidence of
outcome.

    There seems no doubt that in trying to understand the way
decisions are made in organisations we can use all these
contradictory theories that arise at different times in the
social sciences and from a variety of roots; they contribute
to our understanding of decision-making and through them we
can reach a deeper grasp of the activity itself. The theories
are contradictory, but, for instance, one can see that in the
use of the contract system in teaching or in social work,
people are attempting to make negotiatory processes between
individuals or groups both more explicit and more rational,
and allowing for conflict while trying to work towards consensus.

    Etzioni, in his major work 'The Active Society', grappled
with the problem of an appropriate decision-making theory
which can supersede the several different approaches described here, and which were the elements from each –
reason, power and societal structures and bonds. He
acknowledges the limitations of the rational and the incremental approaches: (27)

> What is needed for active decision-making is a strategy
> that is less exacting than the rationalistic one but is not
> as constricting in its perspective as the incremental
> approach, not as utopian as rationalism but not as conser-
> vative as incrementalism, not so unrealistic a model that
> it cannot be followed but not one that legitimates myopic,
> self-oriented, non-innovative decision-making.

A theory of decision-making is also required that takes the
power element and the societal influence into account.

    His theory is one of 'mixed-scanning'. This means that a
decision-maker needs constantly to be considering the wider

issues and their values but paying particular attention to the more detailed problems at the same time: (28)
we find weather satellites hold two cameras, one which takes broad-angle pictures covering large segments of the sky at one time in little detail and one which takes pictures of much smaller segments of the sky in much greater detail.

In other words, a decision-maker needs constantly to be thinking from the general to the particular and back again: to be perceiving the general issues in the specific instance and the specific implications of the general decision.

For a social worker, for instance, it is important not to become immersed in 'a trained inability to rise above a series of cases', (29) the criticism that C. Wright Mills made in the 1940s. A good social worker should be capable of drawing general inferences from his or her caseload in a particular area, and using the evidence that is collected to push for general policy: he or she should also be able to see the particular meaning for work with individuals, families and groups from general policy and from structural analysis. The concept of 'mixed-scanning' must be an important principle in the training of social and community workers and in fact of all workers in a welfare state. This would mean that such people would keep a 'critical edge' to their minds so that they would not just be tools of the organisation, and would not be so handicapped by their ability to see many facets of a decision that they were unable to act.

People in the welfare services make their livings by making decisions in situations of relative uncertainty, and in the midst of complex processes. It is not an activity that should be constantly done without reflecting on the nature and complications of the process.

7

THε individual vεRSUS ThE COMMUNity

I am made unlike anyone I have ever met; I will even
venture to say that I am like no-one in the whole world.
I may be no better, but at least I am different - J.-J.
Rousseau, 'Confessions' (1)

the need for relatedness, transcendence, rootedness, the
need for a sense of identity and the need for a framework
of orientation and devotion - Erich Fromm, 'The Sane
Society' (2)

Individualism is a specifically Western concept: it has been
the crown and can be the curse of Western societies. We
assume the concept to be universal so that it comes as a
shock to realise, as a social worker, that say Asian families may not value individualism and may find it on the whole
a strange and irrelevant idea. People's sense of meaning
throughout history has often been found in their sense of
belonging to something greater than themselves, with that
greater force already being given, whether it be an extended
family and the given role one plays within it, a pervasive
religious faith or a strong political and social order. But
the individual in Western society - or at least the part in
himself which has been taught to think rationally and to
regard himself as his own being - demands at least the freedom to choose the religion, the person or the party to which
he will adhere. And he may choose not to commit himself
to any one of the three, but to live as a freelance individual.
It is this profound sense of the uniqueness of the self that
Rousseau is celebrating in the above quotation.
    Individualism fits in very well with all the aspects of our
present society. It enables us to be mobile, both in class

and geographic terms. By adhering to only one person in marriage, and producing relatively few children, we can regard the nuclear family in much the same partial way as we regard ourselves, and remain mobile. We can be competitive, and the system depends on this. We can split off our private lives protectively from our work lives, and again the system encourages this. The law is set up to protect the rights of the individual, 'rights' again being a Western idea, though now spread internationally.

Individualism goes back in England a long way. In a recent very interesting book, 'The Origins of English Individualism', Macfarlane argues that in the Middle Ages in England, which we tend to think of as a peasant economy based on a strong extended family network, there existed already 'highly individualised ownership' (3) of land, which was backed up by the legal system. The English system was in marked contrast to the much more 'classic' European peasant society. Also, in England, individual rights of possession were granted to women as well as to men. The thesis of the book is 'that the majority of people in England from at least the thirteenth century were rampant individualists, highly mobile both geographically and socially, economically "rational", market-orientated and acquisitive, ego-centred in kinship and ordinary life'. (4) Thus Macfarlane argues against the present assumptions of many medieval historians. It is clear from his book that not only are the legal and social roots of individualism a long-standing feature of English life, but so are the attitudes that go with these characteristics.

That individualism has its costs is widely accepted, even by writers who hold the value very dearly. Macfarlane warns at the end of his study against Third World countries taking on our values wholesale: (5)

if such countries absorb any form of Western industrial technology, they are not merely incorporating a physical or economic product, but a vast set of individualistic attitudes and rights, family structure and patterns of geographic and social mobility which are old, very durable, and highly idiosyncratic. They therefore need to consider whether the costs in terms of loneliness, insecurity and family tensions which are associated with the English structure outweigh the economic benefits.

A marked feature of individualism, which has developed with the capitalist system, has been its possessive quality. This does not seem to be a necessary quality if the value exists in a different context, but it is certainly found as a matter of course in the individualism we are all taught in families, schools and industry. Macpherson describes the original thinking on individualism (as opposed to its practice) in the seventeenth century, particularly referring to Locke. He writes: (6)

> The difficulties of modern liberal democratic theory lie deeper than had been thought ... the original seventeenth century individualism contained the central difficulty, which lay in its possessive quality. Its possessive quality is found in the conception of the individual as essentially the proprietor of his own person and capacities, owing nothing to society for them. The individual was seen neither as a moral whole, nor as a part of the larger social order, but as an owner of himself.... The human essence is freedom from dependence on the will of others, and freedom is the function of possession.
> Society becomes a lot of free equal individuals related to each other as proprietors of their own capacities and of what they have acquired by their exercise. Society consists of relations of exchange between proprietors.
> Political science becomes a calculated device for the protection of this property and for the maintenance of an orderly system of exchange.

Each man must look after his own interests first, which will include the interests of 'his' wife, 'his' children and 'his' property. Property is felt to become 'yours' if you are bequeathed it, because somehow it is the 'possession' of the family: but a person is a drain on society if he or she is given benefits by the welfare state, since its resources are felt to be in public ownership. In the possessive theory of individualism, property becomes somehow legitimately incorporated into the owner's gift, to leave at his or her death.

It may be useful to consider Macpherson's analysis of liberalism with Macfarlane's study of the Middle Ages and beyond. Perhaps what the seventeenth-century political theorists were writing was a description of the actual assumptions of middle-class English people over four or more centuries. They refer to an attitude of mind and a philosophy essential to the creativity and competitiveness of industrialisation and the beginnings of the society dominant in the world today. Individualism is very strong, particularly in England and in America. The favourite English myth is of her eccentrics, both men and women, and of their forays across the world in search of empire and independence. The United States has individualism written into its constitution, in the right to 'life, liberty and the pursuit of happiness'; Lukes in his useful book on the idea of individualism writes that American society is perceived by its citizens as 'a spontaneous social order of self-determined, self-reliant and fully developed individuals', (7) ideal for the market system. The idea of individualism is also a basic part of the French culture, but it is linked in this tradition far more with the ideas of equality and fraternity. Individualism as a notion incorporates a lot of different values. Three groups of the main values are: the dignity of man; autonomy, authenticity, self-development and self-direction; privacy. These values are incorporated into the law and into the administration of the welfare state, though often they conflict with the workings of bureaucracy or ideas about the standard of living appropriate to people living in late twentieth-century society - the judgment of experts about someone's own good. (8) The idea of individuality comes up in such situations as the right of an old lady to live in some definition of squalor (one of Beveridge's enemy giants) and malnutrition or of a person's right to commit suicide. We think children in schools should be treated as individuals, that children placed for adoption have a right to consideration as against the interests of the natural parents and the adopters alike, and we are considering the implementation of a system to give children the right to a personal advocate in some court cases in the future. Professionals by and large regard their function as looking after the interests of the individuals who employ them (though the individual's interest is often defined by the professionals 'for his own good'), and this value is still to be found when the professional is employed by the state.

What then are the implications of the three values mentioned above: the dignity of man, self-determination and autonomy, and privacy?

The idea of the dignity of the human being is most certainly rooted originally in Christian thinking. In modern political thought, Kant's 'The Moral Law', published in 1785, states the enlightenment basis. He writes that all members of society are 'independent centres of consciousness', capable of independent rational activity: (9)

man, and in general every rational being, exists as an end in himself, not merely as a means for arbitrary use by this or that will; he must in all his actions, whether they are directed to himself or to other rational beings, always be viewed at the same time as an end,

And again, in his famous dictum, Kant writes
   act in such a way that you always treat humanity, whether
   in your own person or in the person of any other, never
   simply as a means, but always at the same time as an end.
The implication of placing the individual person at the centre
of concern in political thinking is enormous. The law, the
arrangements of society, then, always need to be considered
against the interests of any one individual man or woman,
given a dispute. This thinking gives the edge to the individual, at least in theory. It gives him the opportunity, even
the encouragement, always to consider the justice of the
system in the light of his own interests, needs and values.
Thoreau considered that it placed 'the person' before 'the
citizen', and opened the way for a legitimate civil disobedience in some circumstances: (10)
   I think we should be men first, and subjects afterwards.
   It is not desirable to cultivate a respect for the law, so
   much as for the right. The only obligation which I have
   the right to assume is to do at any time what I think right.
The emphasis is on what I think is right; the rest, including
the law (never mind the convention), is secondary.
   This frame of mind naturally leads on to the amalgam of
notions contained in the concepts of authenticity, autonomy,
self-determination and self-development. These ideas are
closer to the notion of 'personal meaning' and the individual
person's right to pursue his or her own meaning. This
brings us close to both freedom and liberation. The individual's sense of authenticity has been very important in
the liberation movement; it has gone to self-indulgent
lengths in the somewhat frantic and fashionable search to
'do your own thing', regardless of the people around, that
is held to be paramount over any other consideration by
some of its adherents; but it is a profoundly held value in
Western thinking. It is this sense that moved J.S. Mill to
protest against the role-playing and convention of Victorian
society, that is basic to Sartre's existentialism which lies
in the feeling for anarchism and libertarianism. The desire
for personal autonomy is a strong 'gut' feeling for many
people of different persuasions in this society, and any
threatened erosion is likely to arouse considerable opposition.
   The problems of the authenticity of the person as contrasted with the work of the professional who is offering skills
for the person's 'own good', as he defines it, is part of the
conflict in the job of doctors, teachers, nurses, planners,

social workers – the conflict of values is proportionately
greater as the professional is more sensitive to the feelings
of his client, patient or pupil. Working-class children, for
their own good, are committed to care, then placed in
children's homes which are run on middle-class lines, so
it is difficult for them to exist comfortably in either culture.
Doctors do not tell their patients everything there is to be
known about their own bodies when they are ill, for their
own good, so people may have to make important decisions
without having all the facts. Expertise and self-determination come easily into conflict.

The concept of self-determination is an important and
much discussed theme in social work: in community work
the relative power positions of neighbourhood worker and
neighbourhood are often discussed in theory and in practice.
Probation officers are part of the system of justice; social
services department workers have control over resources
and legislative power. Both community workers and social
workers are taught to be more conscious of the process of
relationships, of group processes, of political and professional values about what is good for others and for society.
Where does this leave the authenticity and autonomy of the
people they are there to serve?

David Soyer makes a valuable contribution to this debate
in his article, 'The Right to Fail', which is arguing against
the over-protective instinct in social workers working with
very handicapped people: (11)

Within our client populations, there are those who for all
their lives have been deprived yet overprotected. They
include many disabled and institutionalized individuals,
and perhaps others too. They have forever borne with a
host of caseworkers, counselors, advisers, and other
predigesters of the facts of life. Certainly, one of their
deprivations is that they have never had the adventure of
putting to the test of reality their adolescent 'dreams of
glory' without first having soberly looked at the pros and
cons with a social worker.

Soyer concludes:

The right of self-determination includes the right to fail
and it is the life experience itself with its success, failure, and in between that is what really enables the client
to evaluate himself and, in the end, to set his goals
realistically.

In this area of work where the power of social workers is
very great because of the physical dependency of their

clients, the plea for self-determination is still very strong.
This is particularly so in a society where success and failure matter. But it is also a matter of self-respect and
self-esteem.
    The need for autonomy is related to that other great prob-
lem of Western life, that of alienation and loneliness. The
cost of authenticity may be isolation. Paradoxically, isolation may be the cost also of constant role-playing, so that
when the roles aren't there to be played, at retirement or at
bereavement, the authentic self has almost disappeared. In
a fragmented, role-playing society, with few inbuilt supports
for competitive individuals, the people who fail are vulnerable indeed. Thoreau, in his criticism of nineteenth-century
American society, captured this feeling when he wrote 'the
mass of men lead lives of quiet desperation'. (12)
    The third idea of individualism, that of privacy, is enough
of an institutionalised value to be the subject of a recent
Parliamentary report. (13) The report assumes that the
concept is a non-problematic one for the people of
England: (14)
    the concept of privacy causes little difficulty to the ordi-
    nary citizen. He can readily identify the part of his life
    which he considers to be peculiarly his own and for which
    he claims the right to be free from outside interference or
    unwanted publicity.
The Englishman's home is his castle. The report also
covers such areas as unwanted publicity in relation to the
press and broadcasting; the misuse of personal information
in credit-rating agencies, banks, employment, schools,
colleges and universities, and in medicine, intrusion into
home life by neighbours and landlords, sales methods,
detectives and noise and intrusion in business life by industrial espionage. In privacy, there is an idea of personal
space, of room in which to live, which all living creatures
require. We need personal room to make mistakes, as
Soyer points out, or to live eccentrically and freely where
we are not intruded upon by some well-meaning (or ill-mean-
ing) interferer.
    Individualism, then, is a value that is both deeply felt in
Western society and which has wide ramifications both in the
working of the state and in society at large. Is the seemingly opposite pressure, towards fraternity, towards community, really opposed? Isn't it rather that the praxis
between the two, the reconciliation of personal meaning with
the need to relate, is the constant task of all our lives?

COMMUNITY

'Community' has become very fashionable. There are community workers and community schools, neighbourhood councils and community health councils, community care and community medicine. The ideas that are contained within this notion are those of participation, power to the people, anti-alienation, a search for roots and a wish for an identity wider than oneself. It is an acknowledgment, made by Fromm in 'Fear of Freedom', that it is hard to be an individual alone, personally to take all one's own responsibility. People need wider means of support if they are not to be an easy prey to a dictator such as Hitler who offers to take all that personal responsibility away. Community is also about loving your neighbour, fraternity, two political ideas that are not much written about; about power; about personal responsibility not only to yourself and to the immediate people you can identify with through the possessiveness of family, but to all people and to all life, all species. Community in this sense is a live network of independent individuals, groups and causes which may or may not be organised, and where people can reach beyond the stultifying littleness of 'doing your own thing'. Fundamental to community is the idea that 'lifts man out of the particularity of his own personal and selfish interests so that ... he is given a less narrow and sectional sort of social experience' where 'the concrete realisation of fraternity and co-operation' (15) is possible. This relates to the original Germanic romantic notion of 'the whole person' who can be found only through community.

The dangers of the idea of community are obvious. Dahrendorf writes of 'the illusion of a community that robs the individual of this opportunity for decision and reduces him from a free person to a bee tied to a hive.' (16) The danger is to become other-directed rather than inner-directed, or at least to allow the balance to tip too far over in that direction. The idea of community can and probably has become a romantic ideal, for conservatives a lost world that used to exist, for socialists the future that human beings are capable of. It is in itself a critique of modern organised society, where bureaucracy is opposed to community, and people do not feel at home in the world.

It seems that particularly in the idea of community, which is both a value and a basis for practice, the contradictory ideas contained in even one value become clear. 'Commu-

nity' can be understood, and community work done, in any
number of different ways. Community to conservatives,
such as the present English parliamentary party, represents
the ideas of shared values, orderliness and the security and
control of roots in the past and in the land, Tönnies's ideal-
type 'Gemeinschaft', an organic unity. To the liberal, the
idea of community would be more about individuals taking
control over their own lives, with emphasis on participation, on delegation of decision-making, on regionalism, on
proportional representation taking into account the freedom
and interests of minority groups. To the radical and the
socialist, the ideas of fraternity, equality, co-operation,
common humanity would represent the true meaning of community. John Lambert (17) explores the practical consequences of these opposing meanings for community workers:
his message is a similar one to the message contained in
this book about working with the paradoxes of this society –
that is, to 'stay unfinished', in Thomas Matheson's words:
acknowledge the conflicts, don't be frightened of them, be
stimulated by their potential.

Community, then, is not a neighbourhood or a particular
area; necessarily, it is an idea – 'relationships among
individuals that are characterised by a high degree of personal intimacy, of social cohesion or moral commitment,
and of continuity over time', according to Nisbet, (18) which
leads to an 'over-riding sense of distinctive identity'. A
neighbourhood may or may not contain such a sense; it may
develop such a sense over a particular issue, and then perhaps lose it again; a community worker may try to foster
such a sense; community care may try to draw on such a
sense. But similar feelings may exist in other non-geo-
graphically-based fields of living – Nisbet examines ideas
surrounding the military community (a juxtaposition of words
sounding oddly to present community theorists), the political
community, the religious, revolutionary, ecological and
plural communities, all traced through the history of ideas.
Certainly in society today there are many communities,
given Nisbet's definition – those of professional and work
groups, those of class, those of fraternal organisations,
those of many common interests, those of family in the
widest sense, those of friendship, those of nationality.
What is missing, however, is often the idea of fraternity.
Rousseau wrote: 'we have physicians, geometers, chemists,
astronomers, poets, musicians and painters; we no longer
have citizens.' (19) From all these partial communities,

as from all the small family groups, many people will be left
out. Communities can become as exclusive as families.
Could all the human race become a community? Could this
involve a respect for all life?
That the present situation is a long way from this is
obvious. Lambert comments on 'the conservatism of many
neighbourhood residents, their deference to authority, their
resignation to "things as they are".' (20) The radical regrets the apathy and the indifference of the populace, but
this is part of the reality of a community. Crosland in his
1970 'A Social Democratic Britain', however, regards the
general population in a different light: (21)

> experience shows that only a small minority of the popula-
> tion wish to participate ... the majority prefer to live a
> full family life and to cultivate their gardens and a good
> thing too. We do not necessarily want a busy bustling
> society in which everyone is politically active and fussing
> around in an interfering and responsible manner and herd-
> ing us all into participating groups. The threat to pri-
> vacy and freedom would be intolerable.

For us, thinking about the problem of the relationship of the
individual to the community at the present time, the question
seems to be 'Is there some way of understanding community
which will enable the freedom of the individual and the co-
operation and fraternity of the community to be meaning-
fully held together'? (22) How people treat each other is
political, how we organise ourselves is about power. Can
authority spring from the citizens upwards?

Part of the problem with the romantic notion of community
is that groups of people with a common interest are likely
either to be united against another group with a contrary
interest or to develop contradictory interests over time.
'A community' offers a cosy vision, but it is necessary in
most communities to live with conflict, with contradictions,
and to live as an individual with these. In a society such as
this present one which contains deep splits in values, ideas
fundamentally opposed to each other and based in opposing
institutions, the reality of any community is bound to be un-
comfortable, at the least. As in the family, the closer any
group, the more potentially bitter the conflict. A homogen-
ous unit is hardly possible any more, except in the short
run.

But the idea and practice of community is important, however difficult, and relates to many of the other values discussed in this book. Participation in decision-making by

the population is the essential basis for a more equal society, equal in power as well as resources; strong local
groups can resist the encroachment of bureaucracy and
professionals if their authority threatens to dominate the
population, and an articulate population is a counter-
balance to strong political government. Both the drive for
more equality and the individual potential for freedom and
liberation are dependent on an interested and aware citizenship, given also the alternative of remaining private, to
meet Crosland's point above. If communities were more of
a reality in society, instead of so partial, and backed by
the value of fraternity, people would not be so dependent on
the family in times of crisis and need, a support which for
many people just does not exist. The idea of community - a
free network of people - is usually opposed to the idea of
bureaucracy, and involves a very different basis of authority, springing from the 'grassroots' rather than from the
top.

Possessive individualism and community are opposed as
values. Possessive individualism is close to the notions of
the nuclear family - you look after your own. But the community, in the sense of feeling some kinship with all people
and all life, could support the non-possessive person, or
the person prepared to share his or her possessions,
whether they be material or about knowledge and power, so
that the other needs people have for dignity, love and self-
respect are met.

8

Equality versus freedom

Freedom for the pike is death to the minnow

neither one person, nor any number of persons, is war-
ranted in saying to another human creature of ripe years,
that he shall not do with his life for his own benefit what
he chooses to do with it. He is the person most interested in his own well-being ... - J.S. Mill, 'On Liberty' (1)

How does either the state or society attempt to reconcile
the freedom of the pike with the freedom of the minnow?
Does it mean they both have to become trout? Is freedom
for everyone unrealistic without some degree of equality?
How are both freedom and equality related to the authority
of the state or the authorities and power existing within
society? There is a complex relationship between equality,
freedom and authority that is difficult to unravel, even in
theory. On the one hand, freedom for all logically leads us
to combat greater inequalities, lest the minnow be eaten; on
the other, conformity and 'heavy' authority limit the variety
and individuality - which may be eccentricity or styles of
deviance or unequal demands on resources - which are
essential to freedom. This is the stuff of politics and the
questions would be similar in a truly communist society and
in a pluralist democracy. Equality and freedom, in their
necessary relation to authority, always limit each other;
but some degree of equality is necessary for the freedom of
all, while a primary emphasis on equality has great implications for the nature of freedom and of authority in any particular society.

EQUALITY

We tend to think of equality in this society as largely being about money, or at least resources. But equality for individuals is also concerned with power, recognition, status, legal rights and duties; it is, as demonstrated in Rawls's analysis, (2) about fairness and about the society's view of justice. It is also involved with the concept of individual rights, as Colonel Rainborough recognised in 1647 at the end of the Civil War against the monarchy: 'the poorest he that is in England hath a life to live, as the greatest he'.

The moral impulse to combat inequality has been well given recently by Bob Holman, a socialist Christian. (3)

As a community social worker on a council estate, I constantly meet contrasts which make me feel guilty, helpless and angry.

A few weeks ago, I sat with a large family who cannot cope on supplementary benefit. The wife handed me a bailiff's warrant and an eviction notice. I had called to ask if one son could have football boots for one team and the other could have plimsolls for club nights. I didn't bother to ask. I had just read of officers in the armed forces, higher civil servants, academics and doctors all earning over £10,000 a year, who were arguing for substantial pay increases.

Last week while getting a lad to school, I looked in his larder. It contained coffee, sugar, and a tin of peas. Nothing else. In London, I attended a dinner for some journalists. Trout, three other courses, drinks and cigars at the snap of a finger.

Furthermore, the most recent figures we have on the distribution of wealth show the differences: (4)

The bottom 80 per cent owned less than a quarter of total personal wealth in 1975; this was less than the top 1 per cent of the population in the same year. The next 4 per cent of the population owned almost as great a share of total personal wealth – just under 22 per cent. The top 5 per cent, then, owned some 46 per cent of total personal wealth, just less than twice that of the bottom 80 per cent of the population.

In this society, inequality exists even without the active ill-will of the people with property and goods. People with more than average assets take from others with less than average, without trying. Merely owning the goods, the access to resources, the knowledge, is enough to take from others: 'exploitation takes place automatically'. (5)

No one argues for absolute equality in terms of goods.
In theory, everyone in England has equal rights before the
law, though this is greatly modified in practice: (6) the
more the actual working of the system is examined, the more
it is clear that the rights of citizenship are 'the foundations
of equality on which the structure of inequality could be
built'. (7) But the general argument is against the grosser
inequalities that mean many people have no chance of being
free. It is difficult to be free if you are hungry or homeless, so the concern for less inequality is also a fight
against poverty at the very least.

The Fabian attitude has been very influential in the thinking behind the English welfare state. R.H. Tawney linked
equality to justice, and linked the theory to the realities of
life for most people: 'the nominal rights of all citizens are
the same; but the differences in their practical powers is
so profound and far-reaching as to cause the majority of
them to possess something less than full citizenship'. (8)

Titmuss, in his Introduction to 'Equality', emphasises
Tawney's concept of the principles which must lie behind
the reality of equality in any society: (9)

> he did not write of [equality] in the naive sense of equal-
> ity of talents or merit or personality. His concern was
> with fundamental equalities before the law; the resources
> of collectively imposed social and economic equalities;
> the equalising of opportunities for all to secure certain
> goods and services; the education of all children to make
> them capable of freedom and more capable of fulfilling
> their personal differences; the enlargement of personal
> liberties through the discovery by each individual of his
> own or his neighbour's endowmen.

It is interesting that this view takes it as axiomatic that
some degree of equality is necessary for the very foundation
of conditions for freedom.

Having accepted, however, that the welfare state is about
equality, among other things, all the legislation and the resources devoted to the welfare state do not seem to have
been very successful in combating the inequalities of the
market system - which is, after all, the predominating
force. The situation does not really seem to have changed
in the last hundred years as far as redistribution goes: (10)

> The first official study on wages was made in 1886. It
> showed that in the lowest male decile [the poorest 10 per
> cent of the male working population] earnings were 68.6%
> of the average earnings. The latest information for 1973

shows that the poorest 10% of male manual workers' earnings as 67.9% of average earnings. So although wages
have risen considerably since 1886, the share going to
the very poorest has remained almost unchanged since
then.

Jordan has shown the debilitating effect of being among the
poor, among people who do not share in the prosperity of
our advanced industrial society. These include not only
the low-wage-earners, but pensioners, one-parent families,
the disabled who are severely affected socially by their dis-
ablement, ex-prisoners, homeless people and, increasingly
significantly, people without paid work. Many of these
people are living at or below the poverty line, as defined by
DHSS. Atkinson has calculated at various times (11) that
somewhere between $3\frac{1}{2}$ and 9 per cent of the population fall
below this line.

Bill Jordan's description of the claimant's predicament is
very clear: (12)

Once a man has taken the dive down into the claiming
class, it requires a tremendous leap to get him back into
the working class again. If he qualifies for Family
Income Supplement, rent rebates, rate rebates, exemp-
tions from prescription charges, free school meals and
all the other selective benefits, there is no incentive for
him to earn a few extra pounds just to lose all these benefits again. If he becomes unemployed, it will take a job
with wages several pounds above the one he previously
held to tempt him back into work of his own accord again.
A family can join the claiming class at the stroke of a
Whitehall pen, but nothing but a major increase in its
earnings can put it back in the working class again.

It was a shock in the 1960s to realise that poverty was
still as relatively great as ever. People who for some
reason are unemployed or those who are employed on low
wages are in a very different personal position from even
the averagely well endowed person materially, never mind
the rich who still hold the great amount of capital resources
in this country.

The welfare services that are supposed to correct some
of this difference in fact often work to the advantage of the
wealthier. Income tax relief on mortgages for that half of
the population who now own their own home is worth more to
the recipient than the subsidy for those living in council
houses; and of course the more expensive your private
house, and the more you earn, the more your income tax

relief is worth. We all have an equal right to the health
service, and this is indeed an inestimable benefit, but the
better-off can circumvent the system by paying for private
insurance schemes or for a consultant's fee or second
opinion; they also know much more the questions to ask and
then have far more confidence in asking them. Most law is
about private property and obviously favours people with a
significant amount of property. The Community Development Projects were far more directly critical of the law and
the interests it represents than stating merely that simple
fact: their report, 'Limits of the Law', concludes (13)
    that within our society the law functions primarily to
    protect and promote the interests of capital. The law is
    one of the main ways in which the state ensures order and
    compliance in an unfair, unequal and exploitative econo-
    mic system.
State education is a universal provision, but schools in
richer areas tend to be better on many criteria. Moreover, our whole structure of educational knowledge is
related to middle-class values, so that children from a different culture have at times a translation job to do between
home and school. (14) This phenomenon has been exten-
sively studied in educational circles and probably explains
the fact that there is still a 1 in 200 chance of a working-
class girl achieving an entrance to university; the problems
for Asian girls are greater and even more complex. (15)
There was a great hope at one time that educational institutions could really affect the inequal structure of society
fundamentally instead of just separating out 'achieving'
working-class children. But studies, such as the American
one by Christopher Jencks called simply 'Inequality', indicate that education as an institution has marginal effect
compared to the powerful forces of the market. Jencks
finds the belief in the possibility of the educational processes really changing society both naive and damaging: (16)
    as long as egalitarians assume that public policy cannot
    contribute to economic equality directly but must proceed
    by ingenious manipulations of marginal institutions like
    the schools, progress will remain glacial. If we want
    to move beyond this tradition, we will have to establish
    political control over the economic institutions that shape
    our society.
The conclusion that we have to draw is that the welfare
system can have only peripheral effects on the workings of
the market, and is ineffective in promoting equality. We

have a society in which it is structurally necessary for a
certain proportion of the population to be at the bottom and
in some degree of poverty; the individuals may change
through the working of certain institutions like the schools,
but the proportion of the population stays the same, and the
relative differences do not alter. More than that, as
Ryan (17) among others points out, we 'blame the victim' for
being there, so as to legitimate the situation. English
society, and world society, patently do not contain equality
in any sense, and show no sign of wanting to do so: after
all, as Rose Fitzgerald Kennedy so truly says, 'obviously
not everyone in the world has two very nice houses, a
couple of boats, a tennis court, a swimming pool, and a
Rolls Royce or two in the family.'

Sleeman, in a recent book, accepts that the welfare state
has 'been relatively successful in establishing a general and
comprehensive welfare floor' (18) although 'the standard
minimum provision has ... been relatively low, especially
as regards social security'. (19) The existence of 'a widespread continuance of relative poverty in Britain in the
postwar period' (20) is, however, undesirable. There are
'deeply rooted inequalities based on differences of family
income, educational and social background in most of the
take up and provision of social services'. (21) 'Once above
the minimum, the deep-seated economic, political and social
factors inherent in our society still make heavily for inequality'. (22) Inequality is not only about resources but
even more significantly about power.

Frank Field in his short pamphlet sums up the situation in
England, showing the combined effect of the market and
welfare systems: (23)

the cycle of inequality is complete. Even in death the
significant difference between rich and poor stubbornly
remain. We have seen that wives of professional groups
have a far greater chance of giving birth successfully
than the wives of semi-skilled and unskilled workers.
The children of professional workers have a far greater
chance of surviving the first year of life, and then living
longer.

These children are unequal when they start school and
continue to draw away from their peers from poorer
homes. The cycle of inequality is reflected in the income
earned, the status at the workplace and in the housing
rich and poor occupy. These class differences appear
again in the differences in health and finally in death....

As Nicholas Bosanquet comments: 'Class differences in opportunities for life and health start at the cradle and continue through the life span'.
Equality is now to be a less urgent aim under a Tory Government all set to compete in the capitalist world economy – in fact, more equality would be a positive disadvantage for such policies. Barbara Wootton said in 1976 that she had 'been pursuing an ideal of equality all my life but had been singularly unsuccessful in catching my prey.' (24) Equality often seems an impossible dream in the modern world. What implications does this have for freedom?

FREEDOM

Everyone believes in freedom, or at least in some version of it – and there are many versions. There is the idea of negative freedom, freedom from all the evils that can beset us such as tyranny, hunger and disease. On the other hand, positive freedom is freedom to do, to follow a vision. Behind different concepts of freedom are dissimilar views on the fundamental nature of man. Some philosophers, such as Rousseau, Marx and Reich, assume that man is naturally free and naturally good – it is a corrupting society that erodes that freedom and perverts it into licence; a naturally free man is also a naturally good man. Under other philosophies, particularly those based in a religious faith, man has to achieve freedom, fighting against a nature marred by destructive tendencies; in this version of freedom, closer to the conservative rather than the socialist version, man needs societal control; his freedom has to be learned and earned.

The idea of personal freedom is closely linked with that of individualism. It hardly makes sense as a value without the individualist framework. Equality is closer to the idea of community and collectivism. The tension between the two streams of thinking is constant. Many people fear personal freedom, both for themselves as others, as Fromm (25) diagnosed; others do not see that the institution of equality, in whatever sense, is justified, desirable or possible. Others find both values of fundamental importance but recognise the tensions between them.

Our version of freedom in this country is tied up with the liberal ethic, J.S. Mill's protest made in the mid-nineteenth century still holds: (26)

not only in what concerns others, but in what concerns
only themselves, the individual, or the family, do not ask
themselves - what do I prefer? Or what would suit my
character and disposition? Or, what would allow the
best and highest in me to have fair play, and enable it to
grow and thrive? They ask themselves, what would be
suitable to my position? What is usually done by persons
of my station and pecuniary circumstances? Or (worse
still) what is usually done by persons of a station and
circumstance superior to mine? I do not mean that they
chose what is customary, in preference to what suits
their inclination. It does not occur to them to have any
inclination, except for what is customary.

The hippies in the sixties and early seventies used very
different language, but their message about freedom carried
a similar criticism. It also carried similar ideas about the
possibility of personal growth, about knowing yourself well
enough to understand the forces that imprison you as a first
step towards release, about consciousness and rationality,
about acceptance of uncertainty and preparedness to step
into the unknown, about the rich variety in people and
against the pressure to conformity. Both Mill and the movement in the sixties fought for the emancipation of minority
groups, both legally and in relation to the consciousness of
the people: both were particularly concerned with the position of women. Both fought against the alienation of playing
social roles in modern society.

The confusing thing about freedom is that it is used by a
liberal like Mill, radicals like Marcuse or Cohn-Bendit, or
conservatives where the word is a main plank of Conservative policy - an assertion of the little man against the
forces of bureaucracy. And the trouble with freedom is
that people tend to trust only their initiates with the gift.
As Jordan writes: (27)

the absence of a constructive, positive, social philosophy,
offering a notion of true freedom and dignity for the
lowest-status groups in the community, is the fundamental
weakness of our present welfare institutions. The problem of freedom and the Welfare State stems from the fears
which better-off citizens have about giving real liberty to
those whom the social system denies the opportunity to
develop a sense of uniqueness, of self, of autonomy, of
worth, of existing beyond the work-role demanded of them
by society.

If it is true that we have to learn freedom, or at least to

grow up in such a situation that we do not unlearn it, any
social system must foster the conditions for freedom for all
its citizens, if there is a wish for freedom to be used well.
The paradox is that you cannot really 'give' freedom: that is
only negative freedom, freedom from. People have to take
their own for any creative effect to come out of it, and then
the consequences are unpredictable: (28)

It does not make much sense to talk of 'giving freedom' to
people. The most we can do is put within reach certain
choices and remove certain coercions and constraints.
Whether doing this creates for other people something
they sense as release, liberation, opportunity and freedom or whether it just puts them into a more painful spot
than ever, is very much up to them and how they see
things.... We have to assume, or at least choose to,
that in the long run more choices and fewer constraints,
less coercion, less fear, is good for people – if only
because it gives them the chance to look for and maybe
find what they really want.

Freedom seems to be the really primary value – a far
more fundamental one than equality, except in the basic
sense of the moral equality of all living beings to one
another. Equality is important so that all men should have
some degree of freedom: equality seems to be a means to an
end rather than a primary value. Freedom – consciousness,
moral awareness and the capacity to chose between actions
and enter into beliefs – is the primary characteristic of the
human being. The person, alone of all creatures during
his brief existence on this earth, is free to examine, to
know, to criticise and to create.

It is ironic that many of the laws that the welfare state
now administers, and that involve the paraphernalia of
bureaucracies, hierarchies and expertise, were set up to
promote individual freedom. The liberal creed of freedom –
'a man shall do as he likes provided he does not injure his
neighbours' – means that much legislation is necessary in
our present economic conditions in order not to injure one's
neighbours. The Factory Acts of the nineteenth century
were inaugurated to protect men, women and children against
exploitation. The Childrens Acts are to promote the interests of children and their parents, often in circumstances
where these interests clash. The social security legislation of this century is to ensure minimum conditions of life
for people not able to procure the necessary basic conditions of living through the market system. Much restrictive

legislation was initiated to prevent people doing harm to
their neighbours through their activity. The intention of
welfare legislation is to promote freedom for all, not to
restrict it: to prevent Beveridge's five giants of want, idle-
ness, disease, squalor and ignorance from restricting
people's personal freedom. The irony is that the full implementation of the vast amount of legislation often seems to
imprison us, workers and citizens alike.

In my view, the practical task for workers in the welfare
state is to be able to operate reasonably freely themselves
within the system, and to promote the freedom of others both
colleagues and clients. The principle of self-determination
is a prime value in social work: teachers have responsibility for the individual growth of their students, not just the
teaching of disciplines. Many doctors are aware of treating
people, not just their bodies. But in order that these principles are not just virtuous words, the promoter of freedom
needs to be aware of and working with the free spirit in himself and others, not just to be moulded by the forces around
him.

Any degree of freedom, individually or structurally, is
hard work, involving more awareness, less acceptance of
the given, more questioning, more recognition of the validity
of difference, more personal maturity, more participation in
decision-making. Relative freedom, in institutions or in a
person, is an achievement, perhaps the only true one in this
achievement-oriented society. But freedom for all depends
on a far greater measure of equality between classes, sexes,
races and countries, and therefore a very different structure
of society from the one we have now.

9

The personal versus the political

Man's condition is, after all, ambiguous and paradoxical –
Paul Halmos (1)

So far I have contrasted particular values and concepts with
one another, in trying to spell out and understand the conflict of ideas in the welfare state. This final chapter is
trying to penetrate nearer to the roots of the conflict between
say, representative and participatory government, different
bases of authority and their relation to the concept of liberation, the ideas of freedom and equality, the problems in the
way we think about needs and resources, the privatised
family and the alienated individual.

In this chapter I am contrasting the assumed relationship
of the personal and the political, as it was thought of in the
1950s, with what seems to be a model emerging in the 1960s,
redefined suddenly with the liberation movements but rooted
back in the teachings of the Frankfurt School and in particular in humanistic psychology. This movement is influential
today in all the social science disciplines, attempting to re-
examine the relationship of the individual to society.

Criticisms of Western liberal democracy have been
proferred ever since the foundation of the system in its
present form in the seventeenth and eighteenth centuries:
Rousseau, Proudhon, Marx and Weber were offering chal-
lenges at points over that period, and though the 'normal'
system being criticised is being constantly modified, particularly by the influences of technology, the thrust of
criticisms remain similar.

The particular importance to the welfare state, itself a
product and sustainer of the 'normal' system, of the new
version of the criticisms, is that this new model offers in a

twentieth-century mode a different way for people to see themselves in society, and a way of combating the large-scale institutions in which most of us work. There is in this an explicit acceptance that a particular structure and a particular meaning to individuals of society are intimately related, and that attitudes and institutions reflect one another.

THE 1950s: THE IMAGE THAT IS STILL VERY MUCH WITH US

There are five major characteristics of this model that I would like to discuss: the idea of a liberal democracy; a capitalist economy; a belief in pluralist values; the scientific rational tradition; and the acceptance and internalisation of the particular central values. These seem to be the basic planks of the system, making for its stability and coherence.

(a) In England we have all grown up with individualistic assumptions of liberal democracy, its relative tolerance and the belief in rationality and fairness – predominantly middle-class values (except perhaps for the idea of fairness in all classes) but widespread enough to make it difficult to find the distance from which to consider the concepts afresh.

A strong possessive strand in individualism, already discussed, justifies and sustains the vested interests that are present to some extent in any society. Possessions are thought of not only in relation to family and property, but include power over resources and knowledge. The widespread possession of these different goods brings with it fear about their loss. There has been a further institutionalisation of property values in the vast amount of legislation concerning property. As Adam Smith stated 200 years ago: (2)

> it is only under the shelter of the civil magistrate that the owner of that valuable property, which is acquired by the labour of many years, or perhaps by successive generations ... can sleep a single night in security. He is at all times surrounded by unknown enemies, which, though he never provoked, he can never appease, and from whose injustice he can be protected only by the powerful arm of the civil magistrate continually held up to chastise it.

In a possessive society, the mere fact that an individual owns more than the most means that the others do not have it – the provocation comes from the fact of possession rather than from some deliberately hostile act.

A corollary of individualism is that only 'rational and economic man' - the man who is both educated and with possessions - can live the good life as a full participator in society. He is the only being who has true independence. The
rest have to be told: as Locke wrote: (3)

the day-labourers and tradesmen, the spinsters and
dairymaids ... _[for them]_ hearing plain commands, is
the sure and only course to bring them to obedience and
practice. The greatest part cannot know, and therefore
they must believe.

The categories of people who 'cannot know' may have
changed since the seventeenth century, but the elite
assumptions have not changed much. As Macpherson points
out, this is essentially a bourgeois conception of society
'which demanded formal equality but required substantive
inequality of rights'. (4) Individualism, property, competition, freedom, class inequality linked to formal equality,
are values closely linked in the system.

(b) This political system of liberal democracy exists
within and supports a capitalist economy, which leads to a
bureaucratic work life for most people. The accumulation
of capital demands large organisations which tend to grow
even larger, sometimes multinational, through profit-making
and takeovers. Large organisations tend to be structured
on a bureaucratic basis whose hierarchy is consistent with
liberal democratic thinking, particularly possessive individualism. Governmental organisations tend to become involved in the commercial world, to take on commercial characteristics and to respond to commercial pressures. The
studies on 'The Local State' (5) or 'Local Government
Becomes Big Business' (6) analyse not only the commercial
power but also the dependence of local government within
the commercial system. The local authorities are one of
the largest employers of building firms on the one hand, and
on the other are also borrowing vast sums from building
societies in order to finance these projects. The identifi-
cation of local authorities with the commercial world is
illustrated by an argument in favour of the new £7m Town
Hall in the impoverished London Borough of Southwark -
'there is no reason why the local authority should not have
offices at least as prestigious as Nationwide or Tesco' was
the general drift of the argument for building.

The vast majority of people work in bureaucratic organisations. They work away from home, in a different world
from the home world. Roles are structured for people both

in the home and in the work-place, and these roles are
split from each other. A fundamental distinction is made
between private life and public life - they are two different
cultures for most people.

But more than this: the capitalist system is at root a-
moral: 'the only value known to the market-place is self-
interest'. (7) Any society with this value at its heart is
open to the most trenchant and justifiable criticism on many
levels.

(c) Alongside the capitalist, bureaucratic and individual
system is a strong adherence to pluralist values - an acceptance of difference so far and no further, and a use of so
much acceptable conflict - again common to many societies,
but almost seeming like a sleight of hand in a society that
purports to be truly free: it is the repressive tolerance
that Marcuse attacked in 'One-Dimensional Man'. Pluralism
as a political philosophy somehow diverts the interest from
the more fundamental to the more superficial. As Berger
points out: (8)

> Plurality becomes a basic theme of life - with this plura-
> lism the creation of an overarching symbolic universe
> becomes increasingly more difficult.

Acceptable conflict becomes functional to the system: (9)

> Internal social conflicts which concern goals, values or
> interests that do not contradict the basic assumptions upon
> which the relationship is founded tend to be positively
> functional for the social structure. Such conflicts tend
> to make possible the readjustment of norms and power
> relations within groups in accordance with the felt needs
> of its individual members or sub groups.... One safe-
> guard against conflict disrupting the consensual basis of
> the relationship ... is contained in the social structure
> itself: it is provided by the institutionalisation and tole-
> rance of conflict.

Overall analysis in politics and administration is regarded
as of marginal importance. Wolin's chapter (10) significantly called 'The Age of Organisation and the Sublimation
of Politics' gives an account of the way in which moral questions are converted into technical questions; how to do it
rather than asking whether it is right to do it all. The
whole concern of management theorists is 'How can we do it
better?' without having to question any more fundamentally: (11)

> The dominant spirit of technical professionalism ...
> determines which questions should be asked.... Moral

and political debate is not outlawed, but it is kept in its place, and the questions which are regarded as legitimate and 'useful' are questions with technical solutions. In doing this social welfare does not only forget its explicit political history; it also imagines that certain questions (of a moral and political character) are already answered satisfactorily.

Pearson's analysis highlights one of the main problems of the professional in the welfare state. Moral questions tend to be thought of as intellectual, academic in every way. Practice tends to be considered technical, not moral. The split between theory and action tends also to fragment the moral and technical components of the professional's working life. The falsity of this was pointed out by Hegel: 'it must not be imagined that man ... keeps thought in one pocket and will in another.' (12) But there is a considerable reluctance to see the welfare system as political, moral or deeply enmeshed in the assumption and institutions of the rest of society.

Within our society, the belief in rationality means that there is a basic assumption that the system is really all right, otherwise some pundit would have pointed it out. All we need is marginal adjustment. John Rex speaks of 'the Fabian assumption that there was a government which could be moved to act on behalf of the people by the demonstration of facts ... an implicit paternalism'. (13)

Within the pluralist system of values the question seems to be, according to Wolin, 'how much democracy can organisation stand', never the other way round; first things first. The society is fragmented in many ways, not least in the way people split their lives between the public and the private, and the system of pluralist values seems to give an illusion of freedom in a situation of great diversity, without being a real threat to the status quo.

(d) The scientific theory of knowledge is a significant feature of this model. Since the Reformation, there has developed a confidence in rationality, in proof, in the testing of hypotheses. The technology created by the scientific tradition has altered the way of human living. We believe in its validity because it works before our eyes. The mystery of scientific knowledge demands a belief in the authority of the expert, especially the technician. Moreover, original science, and its conversion into artefacts to raise our material standard of living, takes place at work and has little connection with people's private lives, where they thankfully take a rest.

The build-up of expertise is called the banking theory of knowledge; it is there for experts to draw on. Education provides the cheques for access to the account. Education is also a culture into which people are socialised: they become different and more authorised to draw on the bank in the process, more acceptable as customers. There is a clear distinction between the educated and the uneducated.

The scientific tradition has a strong part to play in all the social sciences. In psychology, the empirical, testing experimental strand is a strong one: in sociology, empirical work, usually small scale, testing hypotheses, is normal work; political science is usually very practically based, testing political behaviour, and there is a considerable divide between political science and political philosophy, neither being very influential in the way that students think about their lives and about society around them. Social policy and administration has often been descriptive, largely empirical, based on a belief in pluralism, and largely within the Fabian tradition. Social work is generally based on an individualist analysis of 'the problem', tends to be about adjustment, and promotes, by and large, 'a trained incapacity for rising above a series of cases'. (14) The social sciences, like other disciplines, tend to be thought of as work and little to do with people's private lives. Knowledge is thought of as concerned with public and expert matters, and typically with things written down. Experience and feelings are not taken so seriously, except in private life. Rationality is connected with masculinity and feeling with femininity. The woman is private, intrinsically related to feeling rather than rationality, and of less importance.

(e) The particular central values already briefly discussed have been deeply absorbed by individuals in this society, and have to be to make it work. This is why it is so difficult to think outside the values – they are part of oneself. To quote Wolin again: (15)

> so successfully had liberal man internalised social norms and so completely had they come to take the place of conscience that the distinction between 'the inner' and 'the outer', between the convention and the conscience, had been all but erased.

The theme of the organised man is a strong one in this society, from Kafka to C. Wright Mills. Sidney Webb made the point graphically – (16)

The perfect and fitting development of each individual is

not necessarily the utmost highest cultivation of his own
personality, but the filling in the best possible way, of
his humble function in the great social machine.
Herbert Simon, thirty years later, was saying the same
thing: 'the rational individual is, and must be, an organised
and institutionalised individual.' (17)
What is more, the central values of a liberal democratic/
capitalist society do not usually have to be justified if one is
living in such a society – that felt even more the case in the
1950s. The values are regarded as good and, what is more
important, normal. The important thing is then to adjust –
to make oneself work better just as management theorists
attempt to make the organisations work better: 'psychoanalysis is the science necessitated by the liberal ethos'. (18)
   In this society there are two distinct models of man.
First, there is the man who believes in the system and the
values inherent in it. He is a conformist, a position found
in all societies; a position fundamentally necessary to keep
any society going. He accepts the given morality, the given
values outlined above, and the system through which they
are mediated.
   The alternative way of living for people in such a powerful system as ours is to make a split between the public and
private mode of being. Private life is where 'real' living
takes place, and where some deviation from the pressures
are possible – except for people in very public jobs. It
could be argued, however, that the 'Coca-Cola' civilisation
in which we live also affects the private lives of all but the
most determined people – the clothes to buy, the relationships to make, the style of living, the holidays to take. It
is difficult not to slip into becoming the conformist man: the
capitalist system seems able to incorporate most deviations,
and most protests.
   The split between the private and the public does, however, fit in with our view of individuality. Misfortune tends
to be seen as a 'private trouble', quite distinct from the
'public issues' being discussed in society. And the study of
power politics tends to be seen as applying to public affairs
and not private relationships.

CRITICISMS OF THE CURRENTLY NORMAL MODEL

In the 1940s C. Wright Mills seemed rather a lone voice as
a humanistic sociologist. Studies such as 'The Power

Elite' and 'White Collar' were critical analyses of the full-
blown capitalist system.   Novelists of the stature of Sartre,
Kafka and Camus were producing deeply critical novels of
Western culture in the mid-twentieth century.   But throughout the period of the twenties, thirties and forties the
Frankfurt School, though not generally well known at the
time, was evaluating many areas of Western life (first in
Germany, later in America) – the arts, the development of
the personality, the implications of the liberal values in the
structure of our organisations. (19)   Critical analysis, particularly via Marcuse, was influential in the growth of the
liberation movements in the sixties.

The Frankfurt School was created in 1923; members
moved to America, being threatened by the Nazis well before
the outbreak of war; the group disbanded in the 1950s.
Some of the best-known members are Adorno, Fromm, Horkheimer, Marcuse and Lowenthal.   There are Marxist strands
within their criticism of Western liberal capitalist democracies throughout the period, but there were many fundamental
disagreements too with Marx's analysis, which many of the
school took as being too joyless.   Adorno commented that
Marx wanted to turn the whole world into a factory.

The 'counter-culture' movements of the 1960s were greatly
influenced by Marcuse, but their developments have also been
shaped by humanistic psychology, especially the work of
Carl Rogers and Maslow.   Subsequently critical radical
groups, often humanists, have formed in all the social sciences – though more strongly in some than in others: for
example, sociology has been far more affected by the growth
of humanistic or existential sociology than social administration has by any comparable movement, though there has been
more critical work in social policy over the last few years.
There has been a critical movement too in the main professional groups: lawyers have created legal aid centres,
often opposed by the Law Society and the local authorities;
in social work, Case Con was partly Marxist, partly human-
ist; doctors, architects and teachers have initiated radical
newspapers and critical groups within their professions.
Educational methods themselves have been subject to a great
deal of debate in the last ten years, as the significance of
the banking theory of knowledge in the class system has been
more widely understood.

Some of the movements have veered towards an even more
individualistic concern for personal growth and 'doing your
own thing'.   Part of the thrust, however, has been to

reconsider the private life of the individual in relation to society. The slogan 'the personal is the political' of the women's movement means that the most private relationships, including sexual and parental relationships, are seen as political and certainly about power. This means attention being given to the morality of both private and public actions and the relationship between the two. There is a re-emphasis on the morality of actions in a society that has given more attention to material assets and status and the competition to acquire them. Thought is being given to the quality of life, its meaning and its environment, from first principles; to see the 'ought' in relation to the 'is' and not to take the present system for granted. This latest surge of criticism takes its place with the many others that have been made over the last 200 years of Western society.

It was hoped, in the late 1960s and early 1970s, that a change and growth of consciousness, a new acceptance of responsibility for the society we live in and our own part of it, a refusal to conform unthinkingly to the rules and roles laid down and to submit to the demands of large organisations, a move to bring private and public life closer and more consistent with each other, would undermine some of the institutions of society and bring about a smaller, more humane, simpler, way of living. This has clearly not happened in general, though many individual people and organisations have changed through the force of these ideas.

Some of the main, continuing, criticisms of the 'normal' model have concerned the powerlessness of human beings in the grip of large organisations, which few people seem to want and none seems to control. All the organisations of society seem doomed to take on the bureaucratic mode of commercial firms and of the civil service. Marcuse's phrase 'repressive tolerance' here echoes Rousseau: (20)

our wisdom is slavish prudence – our customs consist in control, constraint, compulsion. Civilised man is born and dies a slave. The infant is bound up in swaddling clothes, the corpse is nailed in his coffin. All his life long man is imprisoned by our institutions.

This sense of powerlessness makes for apathy and acceptance of the status quo because it is difficult to see what can be done about it. It certainly fits in with the representative rather than the participatory theory of government.

Gouldner, in his influential book 'The Coming Crisis of Western Sociology', comments on the passivity of modern society: Maslow, Rogers and Reich were irritated by the

subculture of despair: J.F. Glass (21) regrets the lack of
joy in modern society.   Such attitudes are most consistent
with the kind of conservatism that tries to preserve the
status quo not because it is particularly valuable (which
seems very justifiable) but through fear.   It is this latter
kind of conservatism that Gouldner is criticising when he
writes: (22)

A theory is conservative to the extent that it treats ...
institutions as given and unchangeable in essentials; proposes remedies for them so that they may work better,
rather than devising alternatives for them; foresees no
future that can be essentially better than the present, the
conditions that already exist; and, explicitly or implicitly, counsels acceptance or resignation to what exists,
rather than struggling against it.

The refusal to accept our structural powerlessness is
close to Marx's eleventh Thesis: 'Hitherto, philosophers
have interpreted the world.   The point is to change it.'

The sense of powerlessness shows up not only people's
relationship to structure, however, but also in the extent to
which people consider themselves as determined, being only
conformers and role-players.

C. Wright Mills's criticisms of conformist man, already
quoted, are repeated in a seminal article by Wrong (23) –
The Over-Socialised Conception of Man in Modern Society.
He is criticising academic theories post-dating Mill-func-
tionalism and the psychological theories of determinism,
especially Freud.   Wrong's main point is that socialisation,
however strong, does not always work and that is our hope.
The individual human spirit can sometimes survive the most
pervasive conditioning.   We aren't all automatically robots
or controlled by fear.

Criticisms are also directed by writers such as Ryan in
'Blaming the Victim' against the imputation of personal path-
ology in any social problem.   What is seen as a private
trouble may very well be a public issue.   The thrust is
against seeing 'problems' everywhere, and never seeing the
constructive strength that people bring to their lives.   The
message is that men and women could be freer than they
think, less overwhelmed, more able to realise their own
potentiality, the possible joy and pleasure in living, and the
hope of creativity.

This hope runs counter to the personal values engendered
by the 'normal' model.   'The institutions through which we
live are built on the model of competitive, self-aggrandising

and self-sacrificing social relationships.' (24) These
values enable some to succeed in our stressful organisations, and defeat others.

A structured, unequal, competitive society of people
fighting for power produces a person who fits in with the
structure - or at least, makes it very difficult for people
not to accommodate to that mode. Western society tends to
make you into a victim or a bully, or both. Lichtenberg's
competitive man is close to egoistic man: 'individualism is
of course not necessarily egoism, but it comes close to
it'. (25)

Wolin sees us in 'an organisational age that longs for
community' and quotes Proudhon's words: 'to be unclassi-
fiable is to come perilously close to being insignifi-
cant.' (26)

There is a revolt against the forces of organisation, but
the search for community is a tough one, cutting across the
predominating forces of present society.

Fragmentation seems to be an outstanding characteristic
of society today, in living, in the way we think, in social
sciences, in the emphasis on sciences rather than humanity,
leading to a belief in determinism rather than freedom in
human affairs. The pervasiveness of these splits is spelled
out further by Abrams and McCulloch, who discuss (27)

the dualism on which social science is so firmly built.
The distinction of subject from object, of being from consciousness, of the self from the social, of reason from
feeling, are essential taken-for-granted tools of scientific thought. The thought world of sociology is deeply
dualistic, a universe of social actors and social facts, of
meaning and structure, observer and observed ...

In recent critical writings, we find not only a pressure
towards morality - as Macpherson writes, the wish 'to
bring about a sense of the moral worth of the individual,
and combine it with the sense of the moral worth of community', but also a desire not to fragment one's experience.
Many writings springing from the counter-culture express
the intellectuals' need to use feeling as well as intellect,
and to take it as seriously; to use oneself as part of one's
knowledge and to live using the ideas and beliefs with which
one works. In other words, the academic or the practi-
tioner should take him or herself seriously into account as
a subject rather than as an object.

Three writers can illustrate this point. Rogers's 'Man
is wiser than his intellect', (28) Staude's 'much of the con-

temporary social science analyses people's behaviour but fails to understand their experience' (29) and Gouldner's admonition to the intellectual to tell his own truth, (30) all point in the same direction - on that would be a considerable shift from the style of intellectual life at the present time.

The practical message from the critical writers is to hold on to one's freedom and consciousness in relation to the wider social issues in society, not to take the 'normal' assumptions for granted, and to work towards the idea of community becoming a reality. A person needs to work from first principles which are constantly open to review and which take feelings, experience and relationships as seriously as ideas. The idea which has had a considerable amount of publicity is that one's personal style of living should be consistent with one's principles - an idea at the heart of the hippie movement, and one which motivates people to 'drop out' of modern society, seeking a basic simplicity of living instead of the fragmentation of existence which most of us experience. As Brittan writes: 'The fact that Marx, Weber and Durkheim saw no real discontinuity between public issues and private troubles cannot be discounted as if it has no consequence for contemporary sociology.' (31)

The last significant formula must be given by C. Wright Mills in his final piece of advice to aspiring sociological writers: (32)

Do not allow public issues as they are officially formulated, or troubles as they are privately felt, to determine the problems you take up for study.... Know that many personal troubles cannot be solved merely as troubles, but must be understood in terms of public issues - and in terms of the problems of history making. Know that the human meaning of public issues must be revealed by relating them to private troubles - and to the problems of the individual life. Know that the problems of social science, when adequately formulated, must include both troubles and issues, both biography and history, and the range of their intricate relations.

It is necessary for people in this society to be able to see the individual significance of general principles and to conceptualise from the particular.

People need not be moulded by the institutions in which they live: we can reflect on the tension between our inner world and that outer world 'we never made'. The person who does not count himself as a possession, but who has the self-knowledge, the courage and the integrity to say 'here I

stand' is an outsider, but is essential for the maintenance of
any kind of human freedom.   This is also a hopeful position,
'celebrating' as Pearson points out, 'the intentionality,
choice, purposefulness and moral condition of human conflict'. (33)

The frightening tendencies of Western society are now so
considerable that we need many unthreatened outsiders who
are genuinely 'outside' – in other words, who are neither
driven to conform to the forces around them, nor to believe
in them, nor driven to destroy, but who retain the 'critical
edge' to their minds.   The need for such people exists
equally in the welfare state, as the welfare principle is so
dominated and overwhelmed by capitalism.   This 'outsider'
perspective should at least be offered to all if only to help
us understand the conflict of values which constantly rage
before us and within us, and are open for each one of us
with eyes to see.   And if enough of us in many countries
become outsiders, perhaps a more genuinely sane
world could be created – the recurrent human dream.

NOTES

PREFACE

1 24 July 1970. With thanks to the journal for permission
to use this material in the present altered form.

CHAPTER 1 AUTHORITY VERSUS LIBERATION

1 'Injustice', p. 500
2 E. Durkheim, 'On Morality and Society', p. 159.
3 C.I. Barnard, 'The Functions of the Executive'.
4 T.W. Adorno, 'The Authoritarian Personality'.
5 E. Fromm, 'Fear of Freedom'.
6 B. Bettelheim, 'The Informed Heart'.
7 S. Milgram, 'Obedience to Authority'.
8 Op. cit.
9 In Nomos, 'Authority'.
10 M. Weber, 'Theory of Social and Economic Organisations', p. 324 ff.
11 'The Coercive Social Worker'.
12 C.O. Rhodes (ed.), 'Authority in a Changing Society',
p. 13.
13 C.J. Friedrich, 'Tradition and Authority', ch. 4.
14 Catastrophe or Cornucopia?, 'New Society', 22 March
1979, p. 683.
15 'One-Dimensional Man', p. 19.
16 'The State in Capitalist Society', p. 3.
17 C.A. Reich, 'The Greening of America', pp. 16, 87.
18 H. Becker, 'Outsiders'.
19 T. Roszak, 'The Making of a Counter-Culture', p. xiii.
20 Ibid., pp. 105, 17.

21 T.S. Kuhn, 'The Structure of Scientific Revolutions'.
22 Reich, op. cit., pp. 63, 66, 67.
23 Ibid., p. 77.
24 'The Coming Crisis of Western Sociology', p. 489.
25 'Freedom and the Welfare State', p. 78.
26 Ibid., particularly see the chapter, 'The Ethics of Intervention'.
27 'Letters from the Underworld', p. 41.
28 For example: J. Benington, 'Local Government Becomes Big Business'; A. Davis, N. McIntosh and J. Williams, 'The Management of Deprivation'; CDP, 'The Costs of Industrial Change'; 'The Making of a Ruling Class'.
29 'The Silent Revolution', p. 4.
30 Ibid., p. 363.
31 Kuhn, op. cit., p. 119.

CHAPTER 2 REPRESENTATIVE VERSUS PARTICIPA-
TORY THEORIES OF GOVERNMENT

1 B. Holden, 'The Nature of Democracy', p. 8.
2 C. Pateman, 'Participation and Democratic Theory', p. 14.
3 P. Bachrach, 'The Theory of Democratic Elitism', p. 95.
4 'Dissertations and Discussions', p. 471.
5 'Representation', p. 40.
6 J.A. Schumpeter, 'Capitalism, Socialism and Democracy', p. 269.
7 Ibid., p. 283.
8 Holden, op. cit., p. 27.
9 'Politics and Social Work', p. 28.
10 See A.H.M. Jones, 'Athenian Democracy'.
11 'Management of Welfare', p. 259 ff.
12 See A. Willcocks, 'The Creation of the National Health Service'.
13 R. Page and G.A. Clark, 'Who Cares?'.
14 Op. cit., p. 259.
15 Schumpeter, op. cit., p. 250.
16 Pateman, op. cit., p. 22.
17 Community Participation: Past and Future, in D. Jones and M. Mayo (eds), 'Community Work Two', p. 11.
18 House of Commons Debates, 'Hansard', vol. 820, 1971, col. 598.
19 See B. Goodwin, 'Shroud-waving' Staff Frustrated by N.H.S. Bureaucracy, 'Health and Social Services Journal', 5 January 1979.

20 Planning, Participation and Planners, in D. Jones and M. Mayo (eds), 'Community Work One', p. 204.
21 Ibid., p. 210.
22 'Democracy Face to Face with Hugeness'.
23 Op. cit., p. 261.
24 Ibid., p. 259.
25 Committee of Inquiry on Industrial Democracy.
26 Rising Free Bookshop, 'Informal Elites or the Tyranny of Structurelessness'.
27 Op. cit.
28 See A. Etzioni's 'The Active Society'. This will be discussed in chapter 6.

CHAPTER 3 NEEDS AND RESOURCES

1 'Social Work', April 1968.
2 I. Gough, 'The Political Economy of the Welfare State', p. 92.
3 'Motivation and Personality'.
4 'Child Care and the Growth of Love'.
5 M. Rutter, 'Maternal Deprivation Reassessed'.
6 The Concept of Need, 'New Society', 30 March 1972.
7 A. Shonfield and S. Shaw, 'Social Indicators and Social Policy'.
8 S.I. Benn and R.S. Peters, 'Social Principles and the Democratic State', p. 146.
9 W.G. Runciman, 'Relative Deprivation and Social Justice'.
10 'Medical Nemesis'.
11 'Industrial Society and Social Welfare', p. 138.
12 Committee on Local Authority and Allied Personal Social Services.
13 Op. cit., p. 13.
14 P. Leonard, Introduction to Gough, op. cit., p. ix.
15 K. Coates and R. Silburn, 'Poverty: the Forgotten Englishmen', p. 185.
16 'The Politics of Social Service', pp. 5-6.
17 Social Policy and Public Expenditure, HMSO, 1975.
18 The principle of incremental decision-making is discussed further in chapter 6.
19 J.F. Sleeman, 'Resources for the Welfare State', Introduction.
20 Ibid., p. 45.

21 Ibid., p. 47.
22 Ibid., p. 50.
23 Ibid., p. 74.
24 C. Cockburn, 'The Local State'.
25 'Variations in Services for the Aged'.
26 Op. cit.
27 'Social Service Budgets and Social Policy'.

CHAPTER 4 THE FAMILY

1 'The Sociological Imagination', p. 12.
2 A.R. Roiphe, The Family is Out of Fashion, in G.F. Streib (ed.), 'The Changing Family'.
3 'Authority and the Family', p. 98.
4 See H.L. Wilensky and L.N. Lebeaux, 'Industrial Society and Social Welfare'.
5 From J. Cooper, The Uneasy Response to Social Problems and Private Sorrows, 'Social Work Today', 6, no. 21, 1976.
6 See P. Townsend, 'The Family Life of Old People'.
7 From Cooper, op. cit.
8 DHSS, Committee on One-Parent Families, 'Report', Appendix 4.
9 Roiphe, op. cit.
10 G. Brown and T. Harris, 'Social Origins of Depression', p. 135.
11 Ibid., p. 153.
12 Ibid., p. 182.
13 'Finding a Voice', p. 30.
14 Brown and Harris, op. cit.
15 D.H.J. Morgan, 'Social Theory and the Family', p. 27.
16 P. Berger and H. Kellner, Marriage and the Construction of Reality, in B.R. Cosin et al. (eds), 'School and Society'.
17 V. George, 'Social Security and Society', pp. 124, 126.
18 Central Advisory Council, 'Children and their Primary Schools'.
19 DES, 'A New Partnership for our Schools'.
20 Committee on Children and Young Persons, 'Report'.
21 DHSS, Committee on One-Parent Families, 'Report', p. 64, para. 4.1.
22 M. Wynn, 'Family Policy'.
23 Ibid., p. 281.
24 Committee on Local Authority and Allied Personal Social Services.

25 R. Laing, 'The Divided Self' and 'Sanity, Madness and the Family'; D. Cooper, 'The Death of the Family'; A. Esterson, 'The Leaves of Spring'.
26 Quoted in Morgan, op. cit., p. 109.
27 Ibid., p. 115.
28 Brown and Harris, op. cit.
29 See M.D.A. Freeman, 'Violence in the Home', pp. 17-21 for a somewhat inconclusive discussion of numbers.
30 B. Ehrenreich and D. English, 'For Her Own Good'.
31 Ibid., p. 96.
32 Ibid., p. 21.
33 R. Aron, 'Progress and Disillusion', p. 119.
34 M. Poster, 'Critical Theory of the Family', p. 38.
35 Ibid., p. 4.
36 Quoted in Morgan, op. cit., p. 148.
37 Morgan, op. cit., p. 107.
38 M.Young and P. Willmott, 'The Symmetrical Family'.

CHAPTER 5 BUREAUCRACY VERSUS PROFESSIONALISM

1 E. Jaques, 'A General Theory of Bureaucracy', p. 13.
2 UN 'Statistics Year Book', 1955, from ibid., p. 19.
3 M. Weber, 'Theory of Social and Economic Organisations'.
4 See J.A.C. Brown, 'The Social Psychology of Industry'.
5 DOE, Committee on the Staffing of Local Government; DOE, Committee on the Management of Local Government.
6 'Local Government Becomes Big Business', p. 5.
7 Cockburn, 'The Local State', p. 24.
8 S. Wolin, 'Politics and Vision', final chapter.
9 Cockburn, op. cit., p. 6.
10 Ibid., p. 45.
11 In S. Avineri, 'Social and Political Throught of Karl Marx', pp. 23-4.
12 Weber, op. cit., p. 339.
13 E. Greenwood, The Elements of Professionalisation, in H.M. Vollmer and D.C. Mills (eds), 'Professionalisation'.
14 T.J. Johnson, 'Professions and Power', p. 32.
15 A. Etzioni (ed.), 'The Semiprofessions and their Organisation', p. xii.
16 M. Kogan, 'Educational Policy Making', p. 124.

17 C. Frankl, Social Values and Professional Values, 'Journal of Education for Social Work', 5, no. 1, 1969, p. 30.
18 J. McKnight, Professionalised Service and Disabling Help, in Illich et al., op. cit., p. 90.
19 'For Her Own Good', p. 4.
20 G. Pearson, The Politics of Uncertainty: A Study in the Socialisation of the Social Worker, in H. Jones (ed.), 'Towards a New Social Work', p. 48.
21 Ibid., p. 49.
22 G. Pearson, 'The Deviant Imagination', p. 124.
23 J. Berger, 'A Fortunate Man', p. 103.
24 Ministry of Health, Committee on Senior Nursing Staff Structure, 'Report'.
25 M. Young, 'Knowledge and Control'.
26 The Coercive Children's Officer, 'New Society', 3 October 1968, pp. 485-7.
27 In Etzioni (ed.), op. cit., p. 117.
28 R. Deacon and M. Bartley, Becoming a Social Worker, in H. Jones (ed.), 'Towards a New Social Work', p. 86.
29 B. Glastonbury, The Social Worker: 'Cannon Fodder' in the Age of Admin.?, 'Social Work Today', 6, no. 10, 21 August 1975.

CHAPTER 6 DECISION-MAKING

1 M. Weber, 'Social and Economic Organisation', pp. 324-41.
2 C.E. Lindblom, 'The Policy-making Process', pp. 12-14.
3 'Administrative Behavior', p. xxvii.
4 'The Client Speaks'.
5 A.V. Cicourel, 'The Social Organisation of Juvenile Justice'.
6 N. Keddie, 'Tinker, Tailor'.
7 P.L. Berger and T.L. Luckmann, 'The Social Construction of Reality', p. 33.
8 See A. Howard (ed.), 'The Crossman Diaries'.
9 C.I. Barnard, 'The Functions of the Executive', p. 77.
10 E.P. Thompson, 'Warwick University Ltd.'.
11 E. Goffman, 'Asylums'.
12 T. and P. Morris, 'Pentonville'.
13 R. Lambert, 'The Hothouse Society'.
14 J. Hardy, an unpublished study of decision-making in

two Children's Departments, completed at the University of Birmingham, 1972.

15 Nina Toren, Training for Uncertainty in A. Etzioni (ed.), 'The Semiprofessions and their Organisation'.
16 See Joan Hutten, 'Short-term Contracts in Social Work'.
17 'Administrative Behavior', pp. xxiii–xxv.
18 Elton Mayo, 'The Social Problems of an Industrial Civilisation'.
19 'A Strategy of Decision', p. 81.
20 Radbruch, 'Der Geist der englishen Rechts' (1958) quoted in ibid., p. 107.
21 Hardy, op. cit.
22 See M. Kogan, 'The Politics of Educational Change', p. 55, on his comments on 'twenty or thirty years of triumphant progress by the primary schools' which was later 'celebrated' by the Plowden Committees on Primary Education ('Report', p. 56).
23 See Berger and Luckmann, op. cit.
24 A. Strauss et al., The Hospital and its Negotiated Order, in F.G. Castles et al. (eds), 'Decisions, Organisations and Society'.
25 ibid., p. 109.
26 Ibid., p. 117.
27 'The Active Society', pp. 282–3.
28 Ibid., p. 284.
29 The Professional Ideology of Social Pathologists, 'American Journal of Sociology', 49, no. 2, 1943, pp. 165–80.

CHAPTER 7 THE INDIVIDUAL VERSUS THE COMMUNITY

1 'Confessions', vol. 1, p. 1.
2 'The Sane Society', p. 67.   See the argument of ch. 3.
3 'The Origins of English Individualism', p. 94.
4 Ibid., p. 163.
5 Ibid., p. 202.
6 C.B. Macpherson, 'The Political Theory of Possessive Individualism', p. 3.
7 S. Lukes, 'Individualism', p. 29, referring particularly to Emerson.
8 See B. Ehrenreich and D. English, 'For Her Own Good'.
9 See the discussion on these dicta in B.E.A. Liddell, 'Kant on the Foundation of Morality', pp. 155–7.
10 Thoreau, Civil Disobedience, p. 111.

11 D. Soyer, The Right to Fail, in F.E. McDermott (ed.), 'Self-determination in Social Work', pp. 57, 64.
12 H.D. Thoreau, 'Walden', p. 10.
13 Home Office, Committee of Privacy, 'Report'.
14 Ibid., para. 13, p. 5.
15 R. Plant, 'Community and Ideology', p. 17.
16 R. Dahrendorf, 'Society and Democracy in Germany', quoted in ibid., p. 34.
17 J. Lambert, Political Values and Community Work Practice, in P. Curno (ed.), 'Political Issues and Community Work'.
18 R. Nisbet, 'The Social Philosophers'.
19 J.-J. Rousseau, 'First and Second Discourses', p. 59.
20 Op. cit., p. 12.
21 Fabian Tract no. 404, 1971, p. 13.
22 Plant, op. cit., p. 32.

CHAPTER 8 EQUALITY VERSUS FREEDOM

1 'On Liberty', pp. 93-4.
2 'A Theory of Justice'.
3 Politics and Social Work, 'New Society', 6 September 1979.
4 L. Burghes, The Old Order, in F. Field (ed.), 'The Wealth Report', p. 29.
5 I. Gough, 'The Political Economy of the Welfare State', p. 39.
6 See CDP, 'Limits of the Law'.
7 T.H. Marshall, 'Citizenship and Social Class'.
8 'Equality', p. 191.
9 R. Titmuss, Introduction to ibid., p. 15.
10 F. Field, 'Unequal Britain', p. 26.
11 A.B. Atkinson, 'Unequal Shares'.
12 'Paupers', p. 71.
13 See CDP, 'Limits of the Law', p. 32.
14 See J. Kozol, 'Death at an Early Age', for an American example of this.
15 See A. Wilson, 'Finding a Voice'.
16 'Inequality', p. 265.
17 W. Ryan, 'Blaming the Victim'.
18 J.F. Sleeman, 'Resources for the Welfare State', p. 101.
19 Ibid., p. 103.
20 Ibid., p. 105.

21 Ibid., p. 111.
22 Ibid., p. 127.
23 Field, op. cit., p. 62.
24 B. Wootton, 'In Pursuit of Equality'.
25 E. Fromm, 'Fear of Freedom'.
26 Op. cit., pp. 75-6.
27 'Freedom and the Welfare State', pp. 109-10.
28 J. Holt, 'Freedom and Beyond', pp. 89-90.

CHAPTER 9 THE PERSONAL VERSUS THE POLITICAL

1 'The Personal and the Political', p. 22.
2 A. Smith, 'Wealth of Nations', vol. 1, p. 670, quoted in Wolin, 'Politics and Vision', p. 324.
3 J. Locke, 'Works' (1759), vol. 2, p. 580.
4 'The Political Theory of Possessive Individualism', p. 247.
5 C. Cockburn, 'The Local State'.
6 J. Benington, 'Local Government Becomes Big Business'.
7 B. Ehrenreich and D. English, 'For Her Own Good', p. 69.
8 P. Berger, B. Berger and H. Kellner, 'The Homeless Mind', p. 112.
9 L.A. Coser, The Functions of Social Conflict, in L.A. Coser and B. Rosenberg (eds), 'Sociological Theory', pp. 205, 206.
10 In S. Wolin, 'Politics and Vision'.
11 G. Pearson, 'The Deviant Imagination', p. 208.
12 G.W.F. Hegel, 'The Philosophy of Right', p. 226.
13 British Sociology's War of Religion, 'New Society', 11 May 1978, p. 295.
14 C. Wright Mills, The Professional Ideology of Social Pathologists, 'American Journal of Sociology', 49, no. 2, 1943, pp. 165-80.
15 Wolin, op. cit., p. 346.
16 'Fabian Essays', 1948, p. 54.
17 H. Simon, 'Administrative Behavior', p. 102.
18 Wolin, op. cit., p. 3.
19 See M. Jay, 'The Dialectical Imagination', for a study of the Frankfurt School.
20 'Emile', p. 10.
21 The Humanistic Challenge to Sociology, in J.F. Glass and J.R. Staude (eds), 'Humanistic Society'.

22 'The Coming Crisis of Western Sociology', p. 332.
23 In Glass and Staude (eds), op. cit.
24 E. Durkheim, 'Suicide', quoted in Wolin, op. cit.,
   p. 404
25 P. Lichtenberg, Radical Personality Theory, 'Journal
   of Education for Social Work', 12, no. 2, spring 1976.
26 Wolin, op. cit., p. 386.
27 P. Abrams and A. McCulloch, 'Communes, Sociology
   and Society'.
28 C.R. Rogers, A Humanistic Conception of Man, in Glass
   and Staude (eds), op. cit., p. 24.
29 J.R. Staude, The Theoretical Foundations of Humanistic Sociology, in Glass and Staude (eds), op. cit., p.
   265.
30 Op. cit.
31 'The Privatised World', p. 15.
32 'The Sociological Imagination', p. 248.
33 Op. cit., p. 35.

Bibliography

ABRAMS, P. and McCULLOCH, A.: 'Communes, Sociology and Society', Cambridge University Press, 1976.

ADORNO, T.W.: 'The Authoritarian Personality', New York, Harper & Row, 1950.

ARON, R.: 'Progress and Disillusion: the Dialectics of Modern Society', Penguin, 1972.

ATKINSON, A.B.: 'Unequal Shares', Allen Lane, 1972.

AVINERI, S.: 'Social and Political Thought of Karl Marx', Cambridge University Press, 1968.

BACHRACH, P.: 'The Theory of Democratic Elitism: a critique', Boston, Little, Brown, 1967.

BARNARD, C.I.: 'The Functions of the Executive', Cambridge University Press, 1938.

BECKER, H.: 'Outsiders', New York, Free Press, 1963.

BENINGTON, J.: 'Local Government Becomes Big Business', CDP, 2nd ed., 1976.

BENN, S.I. and PETERS, R.S.: 'Social Principles and the Democratic State', Allen & Unwin, 1959.

BERGER, J.: 'A Fortunate Man', Penguin, 1967.

BERGER, P. and B., and KELLNER, H.: 'The Homeless Mind', Random House, 1973.

BERGER, P. and KELLNER, H.: Marriage and the Construction of Reality, reprinted in Cosin, B.R. et al. (eds), 'School and Society', Routledge & Kegan Paul, 2nd ed., 1977, pp. 18–26.

BERGER, P. and LUCKMANN, T.L.: 'The Social Construction of Reality', Allen Lane, 1967.

BETTELHEIM, B.: 'The Informed Heart', Thames & Hudson, 1960.

BIRCH, A.H.: 'Representation', Pall Mall Press, 1971.

BOWLBY, J.: 'Child Care and the Growth of Love', Penguin, 1965.
120

BRADSHAW, J.: The Concept of Need, 'New Society', 30
   March 1972.
BRAYBROOKE, D. and LINDBLOM, C.E.: 'A Strategy of
   Decision', New York, Free Press, 1963.
BRITTAN, A.: 'The Privatised World', Routledge &
   Kegan Paul, 1978.
BROWN, G. and HARRIS, T.: 'Social Origins of Depres-
   sion', Tavistock, 1978.
BROWN, J.A.C.: 'The Social Psychology of Industry',
   Penguin, 1970.
BROWN, R.G.: 'Management of Welfare', Fontana, 1975.
BURGHES, L.: The Old Order, in Field, F. (ed.): 'The
   Wealth Report', Routledge & Kegan Paul, 1979.
BURNS, T. and STALKER, G.M.: 'The Management of
   Innovation', Tavistock, 1966.
CASTLES, F.G., MURRAY, D.J. and POTTER, D.C.:
   'Decisions, Organisations and Society', Penguin, 1971.
CENTRAL ADVISORY COUNCIL FOR EDUCATION: 'Chil-
   dren and their Primary Schools' (Plowden Report),
   HMSO, 1967.
CICOUREL, A.V.: 'The Social Organisation of Juvenile
   Justice, New York, Wiley, 1967.
COATES, K. and SILBURN, R.: 'Poverty: the Forgotten
   Englishmen', Penguin, 1970.
COCKBURN, C.: 'The Local State', Pluto Press, 1977.
COLE, G.D.H.: 'Democracy Face to Face with Hugeness'.
COMMITTEE ON CHILDREN AND YOUNG PERSONS,
   'Report' (Ingleby Report), Cmnd 1191, HMSO, 1960.
COMMITTEE OF INQUIRY ON INDUSTRIAL DEMOCRACY,
   'Report' (Bullock Report), Cmnd 6706, HMSO, 1977.
COMMITTEE ON LOCAL AUTHORITY AND ALLIED PERSO-
   NAL SOCIAL SERVICES, 'Report' (Seebohm Report),
   Cmnd 3703, HMSO, 1968.
COMMUNITY DEVELOPMENT PROJECT (CDP): 'The Costs
   of Industrial Change', 1977.
CDP: 'Limits of the Law', 1977.
CDP: 'The Making of a Ruling Class', Benwell Community
   Project, Newcastle upon Tyne, 1979.
COOPER, D.: 'The Death of the Family', Penguin, 1971.
COOPER, J.: The Uneasy Response to Social Problems
   and Private Sorrows, 'Social Work Today', 6, no. 21,
   1976.
COSER, L.A. and ROSENBERG, B. (eds): 'Sociological
   Theory', Macmillan, 1964.
COTGROVE, S.: Catastrophe or cornucopia?, 'New
   Society', 22 March 1979.

CROSSMAN, R.H.S.: see HOWARD, A.
DAHRENDORF, R.: 'Society and Democracy in Germany',
Weidenfeld & Nicolson, 1968.
DAVIES, B.: 'Variations in Services for the Aged', Bell,
1971.
DAVIS, A., McINTOSH, N. and WILLIAMS, J.: 'the
Management of Deprivation', Community Development
Project, 1977.
DEACON, R. and BARTLEY, M.: Becoming a Social
Worker, in Jones, H. (ed.): 'Towards a New Social
Work', Routledge & Kegan Paul, 1975.
DES, 'A New Partnership for our Schools' (Taylor
Report), HMSO, 1977.
DoE, Committee on the Staffing of Local Government,
'Report' (Mallaby Report), HMSO, 1967.
DoE, Committee on the Management of Local Government,
'Report' (Maud Report), HMSO, 1967.
DHSS, Committee on One-Parent Families, 'Report' (Finer
Report), Cmnd 5629, HMSO, 1974.
DOSTOEVSKY, F.M.: 'Letters from the Underworld',
Everyman Library, Dent, 1913.
DURKHEIM, E.: 'On Morality and Society', University of
Chicago Press, 1973.
EHRENREICH, B. and ENGLISH, D.: 'For Her Own Good',
Pluto Press, 1979.
ESTERSON, A.: 'The Leaves of Spring', Penguin, 1972.
ETZIONI, A.: 'The Active Society', Collier-Macmillan,
1968.
ETZIONI, A. (ed.): 'The Semiprofessions and their
Organisation', Collier-Macmillan, 1969.
FIELD, F.: 'Unequal Britain', Arrow Books, 1974.
FRANKL, C.: Social Values and Professional Values,
'Journal of Education for Social Work', 5, no. 1, 1969.
FREEMAN, M.D.A.: 'Violence in the Home', Saxon House,
1979.
FRIEDRICH, C.J.: 'Tradition and Authority', Pall Mall
Press, 1972.
FROMM, E.: 'Fear of Freedom', Routledge & Kegan Paul,
1960.
FROMM, E.: 'The Sane Society', Routledge & Kegan Paul,
1971.
GALPER, J.H.: 'The Politics of Social Services', Pren-
tice-Hall, 1975.
GAVRON, H.: 'The Captive Wife', Penguin, 1966.
GEORGE, V.: 'Social Security and Society', Routledge &
Kegan Paul, 1973.

GLASER, B.G. and STRAUSS, A.L.: 'The Discovery of Grounded Theory', New York, Aldine Press, 1967.

GLASS, J.F. and STAUDE, J.R. (eds): 'Humanistic Society', Pacific Palisades, Calif., Goodyear, 1972.

GLASTONBURY, B.: The Social Worker: 'Cannon Fodder' in the Age of Admin.?, 'Social Work Today', 6, no. 10, 21 August 1975.

GLENNERSTER, H.: 'Social Service Budgets and Social Policy', Allen & Unwin, 1975.

GOFFMAN, E.: 'Asylums', Penguin, 1961.

GOODWIN, B.: 'Shroud-waving' Staff Frustrated by N.H.S. Bureaucracy, 'Health and Social Services Journal', 5 January 1979.

GOUGH, I.: 'The Political Economy of the Welfare State', Macmillan, 1979.

GOULDNER, A.: 'The Coming Crisis of Western Sociology', Heinemann, 1970.

GREENWOOD, E.: The Elements of Professionalisation, in Vollmer, H.M. and Mills, D.C. (eds): 'Professionalisation', Prentice-Hall, 1966.

HALMOS, P.: 'The Personal and the Political', Hutchinson, 1978.

HANDLER, J.: The Coercive Children's Officer, 'New Society', 3 October 1968, pp. 485-7.

HEGEL, G.W.F.: 'The Philosophy of Right', trans T.M. Knox, Oxford University Press, 1942.

HOLDEN, B.: 'The Nature of Democracy', Nelson, 1974.

HOLMAN, B.: Politics and Social Work, 'New Society', 6 September 1979.

HOLT, J.: 'Freedom and Beyond', Penguin, 1973.

HOME OFFICE, Committee on Privacy, 'Report' (Younger Report), Cmnd 5012, HMSO, 1972.

HORKHEIMER, M.: 'Authority and the Family: Studies in Critical Theory', New York, Seabury Press, 1972.

HOWARD, A. (ed.): 'The Crossman Diaries', Magnum, 1979.

HUTTEN, Joan: 'Short-term Contracts in Social Work', Routledge & Kegan Paul, 1977.

ILLICH, I.: 'Medical Nemesis', Calder & Boyars, 1975.

ILLICH, I. et al.: 'Disabling Professions', Marion Boyars, 1977.

INGLEHART, R.: 'The Silent Revolution', Princeton University Press, 1977.

JAQUES, E.: 'A General Theory of Bureaucracy', Heinemann, 1976.

JAY, M.: 'The Dialectical Imagination', Heinemann, 1973.

JENCKS, C. et al.: 'Inequality', Basic Books, 1972.
JONES, A.H.M.: 'Athenian Democracy', Oxford University Press, 1957.
JONES, D. and MAYO, M. (eds): 'Community Work One', Routledge & Kegan Paul, 1974.
JONES, D. and MAYO, M. (eds), 'Community Work Two', Routledge & Kegan Paul, 1975.
JORDAN, B.: 'Freedom and the Welfare State', Routledge & Kegan Paul, 1976.
JORDAN, B.: 'Paupers', Routledge & Kegan Paul, 1973.
KEDDIE, N.: 'Tinker, Tailor', Penguin, 1973.
KOGAN, M.: 'Educational Policy Making', Allen & Unwin, 1975.
KOGAN, M.: 'The Politics of Educational Change', Fontana, 1978.
KOZOL, J.: 'Death at an Early Age', Penguin, 1968.
KUHN, T.S.: 'The Structure of Scientific Revolutions', University of Chicago Press, 1973.
LAING, R.: 'The Divided Self', Penguin, 1965.
LAING, R.: 'Sanity, Madness and the Family', Penguin, 1970.
LAMBERT, J.: Political Values and Community Work Practice, in Curno, P. (ed.): 'Political Issues and Community Work', Routledge & Kegan Paul, 1978.
LAMBERT, R.: 'The Hothouse Society', Weidenfeld & Nicolson, 1969.
LEES, R.: 'Politics and Social Work', Routledge & Kegan Paul, 1972.
LICHTENBERG, P.: Radical Personality Theory, 'Journal of Education for Social Work', 12, no. 2, 1976.
LIDDELL, B.E.A.: 'Kant on the Foundation of Morality', Indiana University Press, 1970.
LINDBLOM, C.E.: 'The Policy-making Process', Prentice-Hall, 1968.
LOCKE, J.: 'Works', 6th ed., London, 1759.
LUKES, S.: 'Individualism', Oxford, Blackwell, 1973.
MacfARLANE, A.: 'The Origins of English Individualism', Oxford, Blackwell, 1978.
McKNIGHT, J.: Professionalised Service and Disabled Help, in Illich, I. et al.: 'Disabling Professions'.
MacpHERSON, C.B.: 'The Political Theory of Possessive Individualism', Oxford University Press, 1962.
MARCUSE, H.: 'One-Dimensional Man', Sphere Books, 1970.
MARSHALL, T.H.: 'Citizenship and Social Class', Heinemann, 1963.

MASLOW, A.H.: 'Motivation and Personality', Harper &
Row, 1970.
MAYER, J.E. and TIMMS, N.: 'The Client Speaks', Rout-
ledge & Kegan Paul, 1970.
MAYO, Elton: 'The Social Problems of an Industrial Civil-
isation', Routledge & Kegan Paul, 1966.
MILGRAM, S.: 'Obedience to Authority', Tavistock, 1974.
MILIBAND, R.: 'The State in Capitalist Society', Quartet
Books, 1973.
MILL, J.S.: 'Dissertations and Discussions', 2 vols, New
York, Haskell House, 1972.
MILL, J.S.: 'On Liberty' (1859), Oxford University Press,
1975.
MILLS, C. WRIGHT: 'The Power Elite', Oxford University
Press, 1956.
MILLS, C. WRIGHT: The Professional Ideology of Social
Pathologists, 'American Journal of Sociology', 49, no.
2, 1943, pp. 165-80.
MILLS, C. WRIGHT: 'The Sociological Imagination',
Penguin, 1970.
MILLS, C. WRIGHT: 'White Collar', New York, Oxford
University Press, 1956.
MINISTRY OF HEALTH, Committee on Senior Nursing
Staff Structure, 'Report' (Salmon Report), HMSO, 1965.
MOORE, Barrington: 'Injustice: the Social Bases of
Obedience and Revolt', Macmillan, 1978.
MORGAN, D.H.J.: 'Social Theory and the Family', Rout-
ledge & Kegan Paul, 1975.
MORRIS, P.: 'Put Away', Routledge & Kegan Paul, 1969.
MORRIS, T. and P.: 'Pentonville', Routledge & Kegan
Paul, 1963.
NISBET, R.: 'The Social Philosophers', Heinemann, 1974.
NOMOS: 'Authority', Yearbook of the American Society for
Political and Legal Philosophy, Atherton Press, 1958.
PAGE, R. and CLARK, G.A.: 'Who Cares?', National
Children's Bureau, 1977.
PARKER, R.A.: Social Administration and Scarcity: the
Problem of Rationing, 'Social Work', April 1968.
PATEMAN, C.: 'Participation and Democratic Theory',
Cambridge University Press, 1970.
PEARSON, G.: 'The Deviant Imagination', Macmillan,
1975.
PEARSON, G.: The Politics of Uncertainty: a Study in
the Socialisation of the Social Worker, in Jones, H. (ed.):
'Towards a New Social Work', Routledge & Kegan Paul,
1975.

PLANT, R.: 'Community and Ideology', Routledge & Kegan Paul, 1974.

POSTER, M.: 'Critical Theory of the Family', Pluto Press, 1978.

RAWLS, J.: 'A Theory of Justice', Oxford University Press, 1971.

REICH, C.A.: 'The Greening of America', Allen Lane, 1971.

REX, J.: British Sociology's War of Religion, 'New Society', 11 May 1978.

RHODES, C.O. (ed.): 'Authority in a Changing Society', Constable, 1969.

RISING FREE BOOKSHOP: 'Informal Elites or the Tyranny of Structurelessness', 1973.

ROIPHE, A.R.: The Changing Family, in Streib, G.F. (ed.): 'The Family is Out of Fashion', Addison-Wesley, 1973.

ROSZAK, T.: 'The Making of a Counter-Culture', Faber, 1970.

ROUSSEAU, J.-J.: 'Emile', trans. B. Foxley, Dutton, 1911.

ROUSSEAU, J.-J.: 'Confessions', Dent, 1964.

ROUSSEAU, J.-J.: 'The First and Second Discourses' (ed. R.D. Masters), St Martin's Press, 1964.

RUNCIMAN, W.G.: 'Relative Deprivation and Social Justice', Routledge & Kegan Paul, 1966.

RUTTER, M.: 'Maternal Deprivation Reassessed', Penguin, 1972.

RYAN, W.: 'Blaming the Victim', Orbach & Chambers, 1971.

SCHUMPETER, J.A.: 'Capitalism, Socialism and Democracy', Allen & Unwin, 1979.

SHONFIELD, A. and SHAW, S.: 'Social Indicators and Social Policy', Heinemann, 1972.

SIMON, Herbert: 'Administrative Behavior', Collier-Macmillan, 1976.

SLEEMAN, J.F.: 'Resources for the Welfare State', Longman, 1979.

SMITH, A.: 'Wealth of Nations', Dent, 1910.

SOYER, D.: The Right to Fail, in F.E. McDermott (ed.): 'Self-Determination in Social Work', Routledge & Kegan Paul, 1975.

TAWNEY, R.H.: 'Equality', Allen & Unwin, 1964.

THOMPSON, E.P.: 'Warwick University Ltd', Penguin, 1970.

THOREAU, H.D.: Civil Disobedience, in 'The Portable Thoreau', Penguin, 1979.

THOREAU, H.D.: 'Walden', Signet Books, 1949.

TITMUSS, R.: Introduction to Tawney, R.H.: 'Equality'.

TITMUSS, R.: 'The Gift Relationship', Allen & Unwin, 1968.

TOWNSEND, P.: 'The Family Life of Old People', Routledge & Kegan Paul, 1957.

WEBER, M.: 'Theory of Social and Economic Organisations', Oxford University Press, 1947.

WHARTON, E.: 'The Age of Innocence', Penguin, 1979.

WILENSKY, H.L. and LEBEAUX, C.N.: 'Industrial Society and Social Welfare', Collier-Macmillan, 1965.

WILLCOCKS, A.J.: 'The Creation of the National Health Service', Routledge & Kegan Paul, 1967.

WILSON, A.: 'Finding a Voice', Virago, 1978.

WOLIN, S.: 'Politics and Vision', Boston, Little, Brown, 1960.

WOOTTON, B.: 'In Pursuit of Equality', Fabian Pamphlet, 1976.

WYNN, M.: 'Family Policy', Penguin, 1970.

YOUNG, M.: 'Knowledge and control', Collier-Macmillan, 1971.

YOUNG, M. and WILMOTT, P.: 'The Symmetrical Family', Routledge & Kegan Paul, 1973.

Index